B53 001 386 1

Somewhere Else

Charles Rangeley-Wilson studied Fine Art at Christ Church, Oxford and taught for ten years before becoming a freelance writer and photographer. He is *The Field*'s fishing correspondent, and contributes to *Gray's Sporting Journal*, America's leading literary outdoor magazine. He was a founder of the Wild Trout Trust. He lives in Norfolk with his wife and two children.

D1333690

Somewhere Else

Charles Rangeley-Wilson

Yellow Jersey Press
London

Published by Yellow Jersey Press 2005

6 8 10 9 7 5

Copyright © Charles Rangeley-Wilson 2004

Charles Rangeley-Wilson has asserted his right under the Copyright, Designs
and Patents Act 1988 to be identified as the author of this work

This book is sold subject to the condition that it shall not, by way of trade
or otherwise, be lent, resold, hired out, or otherwise circulated without the
publisher's prior consent in any form of binding or cover other than that
in which it is published and without a similar condition including
this condition being imposed on the subsequent purchaser

First published in Great Britain in 2004 by
Yellow Jersey Press
Random House, 20 Vauxhall Bridge Road,
London SW1V 2SA

www.randomhouse.co.uk/vintage

Addresses for companies within The Random House Group Limited
can be found at: www.randomhouse.co.uk/offices.htm

The Random House Group Limited Reg. No. 954009
www.randomhouse.co.uk

A CIP catalogue record for this book
is available from the British Library

ISBN 9780224064316

The Random House Group Limited supports The Forest Stewardship
Council (FSC), the leading international forest certification organisation.
All our titles that are printed on Greenpeace approved FSC certified paper
carry the FSC logo. Our paper procurement policy can be found at:
www.randomhouse.co.uk/environment

Printed and bound in Great Britain by
CPI Antony Rowe, Chippenham, Wiltshire

For Vicky, Patrick and Iona

ROTHERHAM LIBRARY SERVICE	
B53001386	
Bertrams	28/11/2011
AN	£8.99
THY	799.124

We had finally found the magic land at the end of the road, and we never dreamed the extent of the magic.

On the Road, Jack Kerouac

The good sun warmed their shoulders; they heard nothing, thought of nothing, were lost to the world. They fished.

'Two Friends', Guy de Maupassant

Contents

Somewhere Else

Out There

RONNIE SAID, 'CHARLIE, WE ARE *OUT THERE*.'

He was leaning forward to get a look out the window. Our small plane pulled up next to the aerodrome hut like the pilot was stopping for some ciggies at the village store. A guy in safari shorts, his socks pulled up tight under bony knees, squinted against the sun to see inside the portholes of the plane. Beside the tin hut were two white benches, and some dead plants in white oil drums. A big lady rocked her pram back and forth.

'Ronnie, this is civilisation.'

'Get stuffed. Look at it. It's the other end of the planet. Brilliant. Bloody brilliant. This is fantastic, Charlie. We're gonna fish, and we're gonna drive beyond the reach of routine and shit.'

I knew what he meant. Getting away is as much about leaving stuff behind as what you'll find at the other end. My mum said to me I had to go on this trip. I'd been planning it. A magazine wanted to publish the story. Then she got ill. I thought about calling it off, but she knew I'd worry and she didn't want me to stay behind for her. My gran had cancer too, though no one could admit it in her company. We called it the 'shadow on her lung'. As it turned out, my mum died before we left. Fishing seemed like a good idea at the time. I wanted to go away, and this trip couldn't have arrived too soon.

But the trip got delayed because we were supposed to go with Birch. Birch will not commit to anything. He is never on a trip until he's sitting on the plane and in the air. He set the thing up, wrote e-mails to Elwin, but didn't quite book himself in until the season was running out and Ronnie and I said we were off, that we'd call him when we got there. I'm always telling Birch he needs to get his life in order. The man is living chaos.

We took off from Heathrow to Jo'burg on a night flight. I looked out of the large plate window by the departure gate. The light was fading away over suburbia. The beacon of a service truck flashed across the glass. I remembered the train rides I used to take out of London, back to school in the half-light of winter, looking out the windows at all those back gardens, overgrown lawns, forgotten bikes. They gave me a feeling of lonely displacement that was melancholic, but not unpleasant. It was the same feeling now, with my bags around me, waiting to board the plane. Being pushed up against another place can change you. I think change is sometimes the measure of the journey.

Elwin met us at the airport. He carried his right arm stiffly, as though it was welded to his shoulder. He had to lean back slightly to shake hands. I was expecting someone larger, less engaging. I'd spoken to him briefly on the phone, just before leaving. He'd said little more than 'No problem', or 'One hundred per cent'. I thought he'd be sun-dried and morose.

We smiled, and spoke awkwardly about the journey. Ronnie told Elwin about the big guy who'd held on to his aluminium briefcase throughout the flight and looked nervous in turbulence, and I said the back of the guy's neck had looked like a toast rack, and that all three seats sank when he sat down. Ronnie looked at me and said that I wasn't frigging next to him, that Ronnie was next to him, and on the way back he'd play the injured knee card for sure, to wangle a better seat. Elwin's face lit up at this. He laughed loudly, and smacked his leg with his good arm.

'We're going to have a ball.'

It was a long drive in Elwin's backie, climbing from the coast to a parched plateau, inland all the time, mountains in the distance never getting any closer. The land we drove through was dead, like a dry bone, yet people moved across it; a line of them walked through the burnt grass, the line stretching from one hill to the next. One man lay on the road-side, his head on the verge. Three stood at an empty junction, and turned to look as we passed. Huts of duck-egg blue, or brown like dry soil, blistered from the plain. Telephone poles dropped from the sky, fell into the earth at any angle but upright.

In the next town we passed a wrecked bus that had run over the top of a small van and left nothing behind but twists of blue metal and an engine block. The drivetrain had been knocked off the bus, and it sat on the road without its wheels, like a cow that has tucked its legs under itself. A few people stood and looked at the wreckage. A woman sobbed by the railings on the far side of the road. Fifty yards on people waited for another bus.

'Happens all the time,' said Elwin. 'These vans are loaded with people, and the drivers are shit. They know nothing. They'll pull out in front of you without warning. What can you do? It's fuck awful.'

Just then Elwin saw a truck like one that had been stolen from him a month before.

'I'll swear that's my truck,' he said.

'Let's get them,' said Ronnie – he's a fearless Scotsman.

'Ronnie,' I said, 'they'll kill us and eat our balls for tea. Let them keep the truck.'

'Come on.'

Elwin didn't need encouraging.

We followed the truck, turning on to a side street, then again, to a road hemmed in on each side by lock-up garages.

'This looks like a good place to die.'

At the far end the road widened in front of warehouse stores, and a noisy crowd milled about, blocking our way. The truck ahead had stopped, and the crowd surged past. A young boy looked at us, his face blank. Ronnie suddenly thought he could jump out and buy a carpet.

'They'll have some fuckin' great carpets, for sure.'

Elwin's eyes were on the truck. Inside were four young men.

'If there's a dent by the back bumper it's mine.'

We pulled alongside, and they looked at us, and we at them. Elwin waved.

'No dent, let's go,' he said. He dropped the clutch, and edged through the crowd.

'I reckon they would have had great carpets there,' said Ronnie looking over his shoulder.

I looked at him, and he asked, 'What's wrong?'

'You're mad.'

Elwin laughed. 'Charlie's right, Ronnie. Maybe it wasn't the place to buy a carpet.'

It took five hours to get to Maclear, climbing all the way. As we drove into town we saw higher hills off to our left, soft and rolling at first, but leading up to tall peaks capped with snow. We crossed a stream. The sky was leaking away to a dull blue as the sun dropped, throwing the backdrop of hills into shadow, lighting the tops of the trees. I saw a fish rise.

In the morning we stood on a track looking across the valley at yellow grass rippling in the wind. I closed my eyes and listened. It was like rushes dragged across the floor of a barn. A hundred yards away a strip of greener vegetation and tangles of willows traced the line of the Wildebeest River. Behind that a sheer bluff of ochre rock capped by grass, and then off in the distance, mountains shimmering in the glare of the sun. We walked through the high grass and sagebrush, and my head swam with the dense heat and heavy aroma. The air beside the river was cold though, and smelt of mud. The river was low and clear and ran from pool to pool down gravel runs and spillways, lined with slabs of sandstone or deposits of eroded sand.

Elwin took Ronnie down to a long, green pool edged by tall reeds, where trout broke the surface like occasional raindrops. Moses, Elwin's pointer, worked the long grass. Ronnie eased into the cold stream, knocking ripples into the reeds, and lost himself on a trout that we could all see against the pale sand. He'd be there for a while. I walked ahead, found a spot to climb in, and as I did I looked back downriver to see Ronnie's rod bent over.

A century ago several thousand rainbow trout ova were delivered by accident to a farmer on the Wildebeest River. That farmer, Mr Tarr, was as practical as life would make you in the African mountains in the nineteenth century. Rather than throw them away he put the ova inside an oil drum filled with gravel, punched holes in it and dropped the barrel into the river – American Shasta rainbows have swum in the Wildebeest ever since.

I caught my first from a thin lie under a dead tree, and held this perfect fish, gunmetal and purple, until it tightened and fizzed from my hand.

Later in the day we drove to a farm downstream. Two kids jumped on the back of Elwin's truck and he gave them a ride down the valley. The gatekeeper was blind in one eye. His ashen hair fell in tight curls over a face as rough and dark as burnt wood. Elwin spoke to him in Xhosa – a long rambling chat that ended when Elwin gave him a few cigarettes and he opened the gate for us. One of the boys in the garden showed us the track to the river.

Here in a dark pool jammed with fallen trees and huge boulders I hooked the biggest rainbow trout I'd ever seen. It appeared slowly, like a developing picture, out of the dusty water, opened a mouth the size of a kitchen dustbin and turned down. I must have said something, or perhaps Elwin had been watching, aware of what lived in that place. I heard him behind me: 'Don't lose that fish, Charles. That fish is a fekkin' monster. You've got to get him. Look out, he's running for the top . . . he's turning . . . follow him . . . don't . . . don't . . . follow him. Oh shit, he's going behind the bush. Charlie, don't lose that fekkin' fish.' I could do nothing to control it. I had to let it run, and it ran to the top of the pool, stopped at the falls, turned back down, and swam quickly into a tangle of branches. The line broke, and the great trout lay in the shallows in front of us.

'Holy shit, man, that's a big fish. What did you lose it for, you weenie?'

'I didn't do it deliberately, Elwin.'

He smiled, like he'd riled me and enjoyed it, and he shook his head theatrically. 'You're gonna have to get better than that.'

In the morning we travelled further into the mountains, creeping in at the margins of a massive wilderness. The area is untouched but for two or three dirt roads which meet somewhere in the middle at a place called Mochesh's Ford. When we passed it a day later, we found nothing but a tennis court at a crossroads. The farmers here will drive for a day to play tennis if it makes for a social life.

Once, we stopped to look at the valley folding away behind us. Through gaps in the scrub we could see the Wildebeest River. Higher than the gorges that surrounded the valley, the sheer face of the mountain range lay ahead of us. The thin red scar of our road hugged the folds of the land. I was taking a piss when Elwin looked over the escarpment and spotted a large trout in the tiny mountain stream below.

'Come here. Over here. Quick. Look at that. Ah shit, man, it's gone. That was a 'uge fish, fekkin' 'uge.'

It had bolted before we got to the edge.

'You didn't see it? It was 'uge, man. Shall we go down for it?'

We all looked over at the climb down.

'Maybe not,' said Elwin. 'Let's go.'

Elwin wore his enthusiasm on the outside. For a guide, he lacked the weary cynicism that's the mark of the trade. He liked to sneak up behind us, winkle a fish out of a lie Ronnie or I had passed over, and laugh loudly as he did so. 'Eyes open, English weenies!' This was infectious stuff. Elwin fished like the rivers were going to dry up tomorrow.

Later we stopped again, at a height where we could look back and see how the flat tops of the mountains gave way and melted into a crumpled blanket of soft hills. The grass on this side of the mountains was deep and green, and in each furrow of the hill, even along the very top, we found a rivulet of cold water and a line of plants. But then we crossed the watershed, and the land was suddenly yellow and dry. We dropped down the gradient of the plateau towards the Sterkspruit River. When we reached it we found the river corridor was a sinuous oasis of green, with tall grass and poplar trees against the faded background.

We parked by a stone sheep-pen at the end of a long farm track. A gust of wind pulled the car door open against its hinges, roughed the water and shook dry willow leaves off the trees. They fell on to the still edges of the stream. Ahead of us the river turned a corner, slipped across a slab of mossy rock, and plunged into a deep circular pool. Ronnie caught three rainbow trout, one after the other from under the sill, before a black lady came down to the river with her son. They watched for a while, either curious or not wanting to disturb the water. When Ronnie reeled in she started to wash her clothes.

Walking up the Sterkspruit side by side, Elwin casting left, Ronnie straight on, me casting right, searching out every pocket, underneath every overhanging branch, finding fat rainbow trout in the thinnest of lies, we must have looked like cowboys walking into town, bullwhipping the boardwalks.

As we waded up a long shallow reach I saw the nose of a good fish push up a bow wave in the pool up ahead. He rose again, sliced his tail through the boil; then again a few feet away. Elwin saw it too. He handed me a Royal Wulff – a big one – and said, 'He won't say no to that.'

I cast once and missed the feeding lane, but on the second pass the fish brought its mouth up and over the fly. Elwin whispered 'Yesss!' when I lifted the rod, and the line cut a trail across the water. Flashes of silver flickered through the surface. The river was so shallow above and below the pool that the trout soon exhausted itself swimming in circles. But this fish was big – two pounds or more. Its fins were transparent, and peppered with black spots.

We'd walked out of the steeper valley to a shallow plateau. I looked around at the river and the dry hills: but for the angle of the sun and the yellow grass, the place felt like Glen Lyon back home. We sat down beside the water. Elwin's truck was some way below us.

We decided to call Birch. Ronnie dug out his mobile.

'Look at that. Five bars. There's a fuckin' great black hole all the way up the M3 and out here in the middle of nowhere I've got five bars . . . hang on . . . here we go. It's ringing. I can't believe it. Birch . . . yes, it's me . . . Where do you think I am? I'm on a mountain in South Africa, catching rainbow trout by the dozen, and you're in an office in Wiltshire surrounded by paper . . . Birch you need to get yourself sorted, pal.'

Technology has its moments.

It was dark when we got back to the truck. We passed a junction, looked both ways and guessed which way to take. We drove on, looking for a landmark. But for mile after mile there was only black, and the yellow roadside caught in headlights. We'd been told about a collie dog on a sign to a bungalow called Highland Hideaway. We had to retrace our steps twice across miles of nothing, and by the time we finally found the sign we had come to appreciate the scale of the wilderness that sheltered us. The cottage had a light on, three beers cooling in the fridge, with a note from the owners to join them for supper – 'just up the road'.

Back into the infinity. We drove for a few more miles, wondering if they meant a different road, when one of us saw a light way off in the distance. Grant was a big man with the vice-like handshake you learn to brace yourself for in South Africa. 'Come in,' he said. 'I'll get you guys a drink.' Kathy was attractive. All three of us noticed that, being several days out of port. We drank wine, ate roast, and talked about rugby, and crime.

In the morning Kathy sent a lady down with breakfast, and we sat in the kitchen looking out over the misty valley. I was thinking about the way most conversations with the people we'd met had been gravitating.

'Do you ever think of getting away?' I asked Elwin. 'It seems everyone has a story about some friend who's been shot or raped.'

'I guess you think about it.'

'Round Maclear, there much trouble there?'

'It's quiet there, man. But still I guess about ten or twelve farmers have been shot round about, in the years we've been here. Six years. These guys want the farms. Sometimes it's their own workers. It's a fekkin' mess for sure. But no, I'm not going anywhere. I'm here now. The fishing is too good to go anywhere else. I'm here for good, and I'm going to die here, and I'm going to fish non-stop until then. That's the way I look at it.' It seems odd now that he said that, but he did.

'How long you been fishing, Elwin?' I asked.

'Three years.'

I looked surprised.

'When I say three years, I mean every day for three years. Every day. I've got time to catch up on.'

'What is it about fishing, then?'

'What is it? You know that. I don't know. I just love it. I'm alive when I fish.'

We drove on to Rhodes that day and reached the heart of this landscape. I thought we'd just been taking our chances, but now I felt we'd been heading this way all along, pulled by the place.

The approaching road was pot-holed and wet, and the tracks of only two other vehicles were still fresh in the soft red earth, though it had stopped raining hours before. They cut a clumsy course, slewing across the road. The town is built into a bend in the Bell River; whitewashed stone huts with corrugated iron roofs pickled in gloss-green paint, the grid-pattern streets contrasting with the wild river and hills.

We drank in the Rhodes bar, a dimly lit saloon, air like mustard gas and lights that blinked on and off, leaving all the drinkers in thick darkness for minutes at a time. We had two Dutch farmers for company, one with shoulders as big as hams. The other held on to the bar as though it might get away from him. On the wall behind him was a silver cup with a bullet hole through the middle. The barmaid had cropped blonde hair. She was in a bad mood about something.

'What d'ya want?' she asked abruptly. We ordered beers. Elwin bought her a drink. Eventually she smiled, and when she heard we were from England told us she'd love to go there to see *Starlight Express*. I was about to tell her not to bother when the ham-shouldered farmer said he'd love to go see it too. She looked at him like he was holding a turd. He looked away. But when she leant forward to wash a glass he stole a glance. Her heavy breasts bounced under a white T-shirt. The farmer didn't like us being there.

A while later a short, hunched man in grey plus-fours walked through and joined us at the bar. Elwin said hi and slapped him on the back, and I assumed for a moment they knew each other. But the guy blinked in surprise, taken aback.

'What'll you have?' asked Elwin.

'No, thank you,' he replied defensively, sensing things were a bit rough in here. 'I'm just on Coke. Down for the grey-wing, and I'm going to bed sober.'

'Four beers, four slammers,' said Elwin.

'Doesn't hear too good your friend, does he?' the hunchback said to me.

'Pardon?' said Elwin.

The hunchback drank five slammers and five beers. He was going to murder those grey-wing. Elwin was his best friend, and he was so glad, so glad that we were having a good time. We were all his best mates. His best fucking mates in the whole world. He started to cry. He told the barmaid she was beautiful. Isn't she beautiful? We all nodded. The farmer shifted uneasily on his stool. The hunchback went to bed lifting one leg higher than the other, looking as though he wouldn't be able to shoot anything that wasn't tied down. We decided to go too, leaving the farmer holding on to the bar, still not sure what to say.

The barmaid held the door open for us. 'We're having a braai tomorrow, come along.'

'Thanks,' I said, imagining her naked. 'We'll be there. Thank you for putting up with such drunks. You know you really are very . . .'

'Get out of there, Charlie,' said Ronnie, pushing me through the door and out of harm's way.

We walked back to our digs under a clear sky. The stars spun on a new orbit, and the road shifted.

'It might be the Coriolis effect but I need to play with those tits,' I said.

'Monsters for sure,' said Ronnie.

'We'll catch some monsters tomorrow,' said Elwin. 'Some great big fekkin' monsters.'

The next day was bright. My eyeballs ached. Ronnie groaned as we bumped down the rocky track that led to the Bell River.

'Maybe the last one or two slammers were an error of judgement, Charlie.'

'Weenies,' said Elwin. I could tell from his colour he felt no better.

We pulled up to a rusted iron gate, and sat there, engine running, staring at it. After a minute I climbed out. While I was shaking the chain loose, Elwin turned to Ronnie and asked, 'Have you ever seen the snake-dance?' Ronnie said he hadn't.

Elwin got out, and shouted over to me, 'Charles, don't move! There's a snake right behind you.'

I turned. Elwin looked terrified. I wasn't going to stand there. I ran straight back to the truck, lifting my legs as high as possible. Elwin started to run back to the truck himself, with a perfect look of fear on his face. I started waving my hands behind me as I imagined this thing snapping at my arse. I jumped up the side of the truck, and stood on the bonnet. Only then did I notice how much they were laughing. Ronnie was so red I thought he was going to choke, and Elwin just smacked the steering wheel over and over again as he held his sides. When he could speak he said to Ronnie, 'That's the snake-dance.' They started laughing all over again.

We parked the other side of the gate on a high plain. Ronnie got half-way out the truck and fell back into his seat still laughing. I told them to go onanise themselves and went fishing. The river ran slowly across the flat ground, over gentle riffles, nuzzled the underside of earth banks. Only fifty yards downstream it dropped suddenly, crashed into a round pool, before racing on towards a steep gorge of rounded sandstone cliffs and bluffs. I caught two good trout at the edge of the plain – short, stout fish, and both played lively in the clear stream. Elwin and Ronnie stood by the truck, and then called me to follow them.

We trekked a mile or more downriver, standing at last on a bluff over a horseshoe meander. The sun cut across the gorge throwing half of it into dark shadow. Ronnie and Elwin climbed down, and I sat on the ledge taking pictures as they fished up a long, blue pool towards a waterfall. They caught four good fish between them. Every so often one of them would start laughing again. We fished these deep pools with heavy nymphs and bushy dries, pulling up silver fish, while the heat and light bounced off the rocks and made us dizzy in the thin air. Good-sized trout too – all over a foot long, some fifteen or seventeen inches, deep, with tiny streamlined heads and bullock shoulders.

Mid-afternoon the weather closed in with a sudden darkening of the sky, and the temperature dropped by fifteen degrees in as many minutes. Elwin, who knew the weather here better than either of us, got nervous and ushered us back to the truck. Ronnie and I came slowly, unable to resist casting into likely pools, though the fish stopped taking after a while. At one point Elwin was up ahead, standing on a rock, his red neckerchief standing out of the grey landscape, beckoning us on. I looked at him, and said to Ronnie, 'I really think we ought to go.'

As we walked the last few yards back to the truck it started to snow. The snow settled for a minute, but had gone by the time we reached the pass at the top of the valley. We were three miles from the Lesotho border.

On the way back we passed a phone box in a field, made out of sleepers and corrugated iron. We looked at this pathetic structure and decided that if 'out there' was a place, like the North Pole, this phone box was pretty much it.

Two days later, running through the streets of sub-urban East London in a taxi to the airport I was asked by the driver if I had been to Bathurst down the coast. 'Why? What's there?' I asked back.

'There's this big fibreglass pineapple with all this restaurant business inside. It's great.'

'No,' I said, 'I've just been trout fishing in the mountains. They're quite something, you know.'

'So's this pineapple,' she said.

Two months later Ronnie and I were at the Game Fair, and Ronnie remembered that we'd promised to send Elwin some neckerchiefs. He went off to find some, and came back with a collection in all colours. We knew he'd like them. Then a little later in the day a friend of Elwin's came past the stand. He called us outside and told us that Elwin was dead, that he'd been killed in a crash a few days before. He'd only just heard about it. It was a coincidence he'd seen us. Elwin had died on my birthday.

Ronnie was giving me a lift home that day, and we didn't say much. I can remember dropping down the hill to Ronnie's home in the Ebble valley. Ronnie spoke first. He said it was a shame about Elwin. We both looked straight ahead. 'He was OK, Elwin, he was something else. I was gonna go back there for sure, but I won't now. I know I won't go.' I looked at the road. 'You're right,' I said. 'It wouldn't be the same.'

Ronnie sent one of the neckerchiefs to the Rhodes bar, and asked Fred the owner to hang it on the neck of one of the springbok heads. We've not been back to see if it's there.

Magic Thunderbolt
of Wisdom

THE PHONE RANG. 'GET YOUR PASSPORT OUT, WE'RE going to the Himalayas to catch trout.'

'Hello, Patrick. Nice to hear from you.' He likes to call up like this. No hellos, right into the subject. It's usually something about where we ought to be going fishing, or where he's just been, but not often as exotic as this. Or there'll be a silence. He'll act amazed that I've picked up the phone at all, announce that he's finally got hold of me.

I have to admit I've been difficult to reach lately. I've decided the phone is a cancer that eats your soul. I can't sit down to write for more than an hour without finding some excuse to let my life leak away down the phone line. So I try to ignore it. It's impossible, of course. I've turned the ringer off, but I'm the worst offender. I let the beast out, thinking a little walk won't hurt, and before I know it's off the lead, shitting in the hall, chewing the furniture. Silence lets you make sense of things, but I catch myself doing anything I can to get away from it. I fill my life with noise, banging drums on the edge of the abyss. All this was running around my head and getting me down, and I knew it was time to take off, and go fishing.

Ironic that it took a phone call. Only a few weeks before, I'd found a drawing in a Victorian book. It showed a perfect upland brown trout, in detail down to the teeth and the spots on the adipose fin, caught in the Nilgiri Hills of Madras back in the 1860s. I took a photocopy, pinned it on the wall, and thought about the journey that trout would have taken: an egg packed in ice on a steamer out of some port like Liverpool, the ice-packs hauled overland by teams of ponies, to a river in the mountains. I tried to imagine the stream the trout came from, running through dry red earth, overhung with trees, but had to create my idea of the place from packets of PG Tips, or those prints in curry restaurants: green hills through the windows of a room in which lovers kiss, his hand on her breast, toes curled. In my imagined Madras the trout rose at locusts.

'When?' I asked.

Patrick said we should meet up to plan the trip. His friend Rod could get us into Bhutan, a remote kingdom on the southern slopes of the Himalayas. It was not exactly impossible for a foreigner to get into Bhutan, but it was difficult. Rod knew a few important people there, though. He could pull strings. The place was cut through with trout streams, and only the King bothered with them. We'd have his permission. Rod was getting married; Bhutan was his honeymoon. He'd go out early, spend a week in the mountains with Alison, and then we'd join them.

I met Rod and Alison in a London pub the night we planned the trip. Sarah was there too – she'd be coming along with Patrick. It was raining outside – a cold February day. As we talked about Bhutan, the thought of escaping this depressing winter grew more and more appealing. The trip was sketched out. To get to Bhutan we had to travel through Calcutta.

Nothing will prepare you for Calcutta. As we climbed out of the plane, heat rolled off the runway in waves, like breakers off a hot sea. Patrick, dressed for a shitty day in London, stripped down to his shirt before our shoes hit the sticky tarmac. The airport building was incredibly hot, claustrophobic and airless, heaving with people. Officials with dog tags in grubby white uniforms ushered queues left then right. It took hours to get through the building, lining up, filling in forms, back to the beginning, queuing here not there, there not here. A skeletal lady came to the window. She saw me and held out her sick baby, begged me to pass a coin under the door. I only had dollar bills. I slipped one through the gap. A mistake. We were overwhelmed.

Patrick meanwhile was circulating the foyer with a taxi pirate.

'When did Patrick last fly anywhere?' I asked Sarah.

'Doesn't get out of Monmouth that often.'

Patrick unfolded his money asking how much, and the driver's eyes widened. I walked over and tried to make it clear we wanted a licensed cab, and nothing else, and the driver in frustration walked into the cab office and stuck his head through the window to continue the argument. The officer inside started to shout at him, but he held on, his head stuck out through the hole in the mesh, in the end imploring us to take his cab. At last he walked away, shrugging off the grabbing hands of the taxi officer, saying he was not at all happy with us. We left with a slip of paper for government-licensed taxi no. 8897, and outside people fought to touch our luggage as it was loaded, then held out their hands, desperate. We gave money, and it brought more people, all begging. At last we sat in the taxi, staring ahead, trying not to notice the beggars or our nagging sense of shame.

In the end all we saw of Calcutta we saw through the window of our cab, a rusty Austin Ambassador, yellow like all the others that swarmed the wide but laneless highway which led into the city centre. The driver leant his elbow on the horn, and the whole dumb herd lowed like electric cattle at sunset. Heat poured in the windows, along with choking dust and fumes. We passed children playing in gutters, men hammering aimlessly at lumps of concrete, crows fighting over rubbish. The suburbs rose out of a swamp – half-finished buildings, waist deep in water;

white egrets on the edges of ponds; a stinking river. The buildings and streets closed in. The city condensed, and in its compression of ornate architecture and improvised shacks we found the Fairlawn Hotel, an oasis of fading colonialism, which we were relieved to hide in, though we wouldn't have admitted it.

We sat and drank beer. Crows argued in the trees overhead. The sound of busy traffic echoed off the tall buildings all around. A dull, belching roar. Patrick and I walked to the gate, and looked both ways down the clogged Calcutta street. A look at life in another dimension. We hesitated on the pavement. For some reason we stayed inside the gate, and looked forward to Bhutan. Calcutta was our River Styx, and in the morning our ferryman in his yellow Ambassador took us back across the river.

The runway at Paro is laid down on one of the few flat valleys in Bhutan where there is room enough to land a plane. Even so we dropped like a Stuka. My stomach lurched upwards and I needed a piss. I got the feeling I was spinning down a hole in the surface of the earth, until the plane eased out of its dive, with the mountains all around us. The river below carried a tinge of colour, a milky white. It meandered across a plain of dry boulders, running underneath the massive walls of a temple which reared from the ground up to an elaborate golden roofline. The temple itself was pressed up against the side of a hill that climbed to a steep ridge. The ridge ran away up the valley, beyond sight, up and up. All around stands of wooden poles with silk flags shook in the breeze.

Karma, our guide, met us at the airport. He told us they were prayer flags. Karma was helplessly polite, bowing and grinning, running to and fro with our luggage, throwing bags into the back of a blue Toyota. At the wheel sat Mindu chewing betel nut, his smile revealing a row of bright red teeth. The road to Thimphu was dusty and hot, crowded with mini-vans, or chromed timber trucks with outlandish eyes painted over the headlights.

We found Rod and Alison in the bar of the Drak Hotel on Thimphu's Central Square. Rod ordered up five bottles of Golden Eagle, knocked the necks together, and drank.

'Here's to the trout of Bhutan.'

Kencho, our head guide, sat stiff in the corner in his purple gho, socks pulled up above stout shoes. He told us what we wanted to hear – that the rivers were all teeming with gigantic trout. With that we went to bed early, but keyed up on the thrill of travel I slept fitfully, and dreamt about a vast fish, half-trout, half-catfish, singing in a nightclub. I woke in a sweat. Out in the dark, Thimpu's dogs howled to each other across the empty streets. Hundreds of them wailed endlessly into the night – a terrible noise.

'Those dogs were something,' I said wearily over breakfast.

'They won't kill the things because they're Buddhists,' yawned Alison.

'I just dreamt of catapults,' said Patrick.

It was time to go. We needed to fish soon. On the way up the road had followed a river, every turn and pool of which drove Patrick and me crazy to stop the truck, string a rod and walk in. Now Kencho meant us to leave this valley behind and travel for another day. He sensed our desperation but assured us that we'd find trout over the mountain pass. We'd spend ten days on the road, unpacking each night at guesthouses, even camping by the rivers, exploring all the valleys that divide Bhutan like furrows. We'd have plenty of time to fish, he said.

The country stretches east to west but the valleys run north to south. Any drive from one river to the next involves precipitous climbs on single-lane roads – roads that sometimes get washed away by landslides. Mindu sat at the wheel of his Toyota pick-up, chewing betel nut, tapping to oriental funk playing loudly in the cab. First stop was Dochu La, a misty gap in the mountains, noticeably colder than the valley floor we'd left behind. Two drivers, two guides and a cook, all uniformed in ghos, and three fishermen in jeans lined up along the road and pissed into the rhododendrons. Alison and Sarah went deeper into the bushes. Above us, torn prayer flags flapped in the breeze. Kencho, nudging Rod in the ribs, said that Karma was a virgin.

Mindu laughed, and spat betel nut juice on the ground.

'Lama Drukpa Kunley was the Divine Madman,' said Karma, shaking off the drops. 'With his magic thunderbolt of wisdom he subdued the demoness who hid at this pass and ate travellers.'

'His magic thunderbolt of wisdom wouldn't happen to have been his penis, would it?' asked Rod. Rod knew all about Bhutanese mythology.

Karma grinned, and carried on. 'He killed her by making it as large as possible. He put it in her mouth, but then she turned into a dog.' Karma shrugged. 'So, he dragged her down the mountain. By the time he got to the bottom she had disappeared, so he built a temple called the temple of the lost dog. Now childless women go to the temple and sit on a large phallus to receive a wang from the saint. A wang is a blessing.'

'It's true,' said Kencho.

'Sure,' I said, zipping up. 'We call it a blessing where we come from too.'

'He had it all worked out anyway,' added Patrick. 'What, these teethmarks, darling? You'll never guess but . . .'

We left Dochu La and crossed over the pass to Punakha. The road dropped away, no wider than the truck, sheer edges falling hundreds of feet below the wheels. The air became hotter. We stripped back to T-shirts as the trucks descended. It seemed odd to start our search in this heat, but here climates are stacked one on top of the next. The Punakha Chhu snaked below us, an ochre ribbon cutting through scrub grassland and terraced meadows. It starts in the Himalayan foothills, feeding icy water to the dry plain of Punakha. From high up the pass we had seen that the river was coloured by heavy rain, so we turned upstream to find the Mo Chhu, a smaller tributary which Kencho was sure would run clear. 'You wait,' he said. 'You'll see that this stream is clear. It's always clear. Never coloured. I have never seen this stream coloured. Impossible.' But the Mo Chhu swung against the bluff below us, milky white. Kencho slapped his head over and over, cursing the weather, until there was a red mark above his eyebrows.

'Hey, chill out, Kencho,' said Rod. But Kencho wouldn't talk. We pulled in by a side stream, and agreed to fish anyway. We found a beach and strung up the rods on the sandy shore, eyes on the water. It looked hopeless. The coloured river curved towards us, a powerful rip through the middle of the channel. As we sat there wondering what to do next a vast fish leapt high in the air. Time and the fish held still for a moment, suspended.

'Was that a trout? Are we sure that was a trout?' Patrick broke the silence.

'Sure,' said Kencho, smiling now, shrugging his shoulders like he'd never expected anything else. We watched the river again. Way out in the middle a trout boiled at the surface, then another feeding further down the central rip. Another a moment later. They were a long way out and the flow was treacherous, but a very good cast might just reach those fish nearest us. Again one left the water entirely, the splash loud enough for us to start believing Kencho's stories of 'very, very big fish'. But in four hours of casting none of us found out what they were taking. I ran through the fly box: olives, sedges, smuts – the lot. Most casts fell short; a few made the channel, but dragged quickly. 'Could be the fly, could be the drag. Who knows?' I said. Patrick sat on a boulder nearby, smoking, watching the fish. I scooped at the milky water where it ran under our bank and held a pool of water in my palms. A small black insect spun vigorously against the surface tension. I showed Patrick. 'It's easy,' I said. 'We need clockwork flies.'

'Bollocks,' said Patrick. 'Let's go and get a beer.'

We left the stream late afternoon, and a thick fog curled in over the trees. Mindu had been asleep in the truck or chewing beetle nut for most of the day. I'd seen what beetle nut does for driving in New Guinea years before. A caffeinated euphoria kicks in, followed by an overwhelming need to sleep. We were at the sleepy part and the fog was soporific too. Patrick dozed off, but I was ready to jump for my life. Even Rod did up his seat belt. Mindu grinned his red teeth at us, but his eyelids were heavy, so we kept him awake singing songs, joking about the magic thunderbolt and teaching him how to swear in English.

We found a candlelit village pub opposite a temple

which straddled the junction of the Mo Chhu and the Punakha Chhu. On the wall I noticed a poster: a utopian cityscape from the Sixties. But the age of the image interested me less than its colours: electric tangerine, and false, like a television. And suddenly I noticed the absence of this electronic nipple. 'This is brilliant!' I said, distracting the others. 'No telly. No computers. No telephones. These guys paint cocks and fannies all over their buildings. They're completely unrepressed.'

Outside the pub teenage monks in purple vestments played a game of football. The street was busy with children. One stopped at the pub window, took a look at us and ran away. Moments later he came back with a group of friends who peered in one by one, hiding whenever we waved or spoke. After a while they came inside, slowly, timidly, backs to the counter. Patrick sparked his cigarette lighter, and they ran giggling to hide behind the beer crates. The bravest came out first, and asked to see the lighter. The littlest of them hid behind his legs.

I caught my first Bhutanese trout from the stream by Chendebji Chorten – a remote prayer house in the hills. Rod and Patrick were downriver. I had clambered upstream to a deep pool. I flicked a big dry fly across the channel, and let it ride the current along the edge. Nothing. I held the rod high and teased the fly across the surface. Still nothing. The spot was perfect for a fish, so I tied on a stonefly nymph and

threw it upstream. The fly wasn't heavy enough –
it washed back through the turbulent water. I knotted six inches of nylon to the gape of this fly, and
tied on another. This time with enough weight the
nymphs sank to the bottom, and I tried the run
again. The line straightened upriver, inert then alive.
The trout found the current, turned with it, a bright
flash in the stream. She cut an angle across the flow,
passed me under the rod tip, and tore though both
pools, on over the edge, line ripping from my fly
reel. I caught up with her in the shallows of the next
pool downriver, held her over the stones for a
moment, remembering the trout from the Nilgiri
Hills. This one was over a foot long, nut brown
with silver sides, and polished clean and hard, like
the boulders.

We caught a lot that day, all on nymphs. Only at
last light, when a handful of olives drifted off the
surface, did the trout start to rise. Most were small,
nothing like the size of the fish we'd seen in the
Mo Chhu, yet they were wild fish and, like us, a
long way from home – this stream could have been
flowing through the uplands of central Wales. And
yet the differences crept in at the edge of perception
– the bamboo bridge; the cowbells; the prayer flags;
the watchful eyes painted on to the walls of the
prayer house. We ended the day sitting by the bridge
while three children held hands and stared at us, the
smallest with a big ball of snot under his nose that
inflated and deflated as he breathed. When Patrick

shouted 'Yak butter cheese!' they giggled uncontrollably, and the bubble burst.

Another pass, another heavy drive. Too much driving. You don't acquire a place by passing through it. It's more like erosion – a little rubs off. And for a little to rub off, a little must be worn away. Hotels get built, culture gets packaged. I've never been anywhere that programme is less advanced than Bhutan, though it's happening here too. But as we travelled west the apparatus of twentieth-century brain death fell away. The place is cut off. Wherever we slept the dogs howled all night. Out here in the middle of nowhere I heard them from across the valley, miles away. One long howl, answered by another, then another closer still, until the dog under my window was singing with twenty others across ten miles of open country. I leant out the window. 'Hey mutt, wherever you are, SHUT UP!' But after a few nights I got used to it. What else could I do? I read my book by candlelight until it fell from my hands, and the dogs howled through my sleep. Those dogs did something else too. Their howling described the distance of the night. In that distance I felt comfortingly insignificant.

Mindu and Kencho would not leave Karma alone about his virginity. Karma was bright. But he knew nothing about women. Kencho was married but as far as we could tell he had a girlfriend in every valley – the mountain ranges obviously a psychological barrier and some kind of physical insurance against getting a frying pan on the back of the head. With Mindu I guessed it was as much bluff as anything else. He didn't look any more a man of the world than Karma. Ugyen, our cook, didn't join in the teasing. He smiled at the jokes, but occasionally he took Karma aside and spoke to him, and Karma listened intently.

We made for the Tang valley in the north-eastern corner of Bhumtang province, two hours up a rough dirt track. 'The girls are pretty and the trout are big in this province,' said Kencho, rubbing his hands. There was little doubt about which thought excited him most. We pulled up at a small shop by the road-side, to get a drink. The shop, with its musty, dark interior that smelt of rubber sneakers, sold textiles – piles of silk and prayer flags. We drank our Coke in the sun, leaning against the trucks, appreciating the break. In a lean-to shed beside the shop five girls sat at looms, weaving. Kencho and Mindu strolled over to them. Kencho started to talk. Karma hovered in the background, slightly embarrassed. There was a good deal of bravura to the show, Kencho letting us know he was some kind of dude, us laughing, egging him on. Suddenly Ugyen was sitting on a stool beside the prettiest of them, as close as if they'd known each other for ever. He whispered in her ear. She giggled and blushed.

'Hey, Dr Luurve,' said Rod. 'How did he get there? Now that is style, Kencho, that is a smooth operator.'

Kencho backed away, shrugging his shoulders. 'He always gets the girls.'

'Well, he can cook,' said Alison. 'What do you expect?'

'Tonight, though,' said Kencho. 'Tonight we are camping in the Tang valley. Tonight is for night-hunting.'

Patrick was anxious to get to the river. 'Hey, Dr Luurve. We've got to go.' Ugyen peeled himself away with a phrase that had the girl hiding behind her hair. He ran back to the truck, jumped in and said, 'Let's go.' He never looked back.

The Tang Chhu cuts through dry red earth, running down steep cascades of rock into pools under cliffs. Tangles of trees lay in broken piles, smashed by floodwater against the boulders beside the stream, bleached white in the sun. The boulders were clean white too, and perfectly round. Kencho claimed to have caught big fish here. The stream looked as though it would hold them. A few grasshoppers scattered on to the surface as we walked down to the stream. At the edge, along the rocks at the lip of a continuous line of encrusted, dry algae that marked a point from which the river had shrunk, we found hundreds of desiccated stonefly nymphs.

The water was cold, despite the hot day and burning sun. We drifted downriver, hopscotch fishing, covering the water quickly. There was little hatching, and the fishing was slow at first. I found the deepest pool, and tried my stonefly nymph again, on a long leader, to get the fly down. I threw the line upriver and allowed the nymph to sink all the way to the bottom, throwing mends into the line to counter the drag of the surface current. The fly dropped down a gulley between rocks, snagged momentarily, then came loose. It snagged again, and the line tightened into the log or rock my fly had found. But then the rock moved. The line tightened further and the rod bent over, though I wasn't pulling. It must be a fish. Suddenly the rod snapped against the surface, then lifted as the fish turned upwards against the resistance and came into the air. Water flicked off it in the bright light, the trout hanging there for a second, crashing back down with a smack. A massive trout. I had no net. Patrick sat downriver from me, studying the fight, smoking his cigarette. 'It doesn't really count, you know. You hooked it with a nymph. You can land it.'

'Patrick. You're a bastard. And a deluded dry fly snob.'

The trout had sounded again, and rolling in big circles across the bottom of the pool, it made a pass along the shore close to me, two feet down as it rode the gravel edge. Turning back into the pool, it vanished into the darker water. Moments after it had gone, the surface rolled gently above the line of its passage. Shit, it was big. Finally I tricked it into a small pool at the base of a rill that ran into the river from the hill above us. The trout was as long as my forearm.

'Hey Patrick. Want a stonefly nymph? I have a few spare.'

'Get lost.'

Two small boys in red boots followed us. They never came close. When I pulled out a camera they posed formally. They looked at us intently, amazed at the Polaroids, Gore-Tex and graphite. Later in the day we saw them again, waving bamboo canes back and forth, hopscotching along the banks of the river.

Patrick, Rod and I did the same all afternoon, covering miles of water. Long riffles separated the pools, but the best spots were the shallow runs of even depth broken by boulders. A species of small olive hatched in waves on and off during the day, and the trout rose at them enthusiastically. From a rocky shore under thorn bushes, where I sat down to cool off and take some pictures, Patrick hooked into a good fish. I got a shot of Patrick holding it up, and looking at it now the picture is perfectly exposed but for the fish, so bright that it shines off the film.

We camped beside the river, made a fire out of driftwood. We had brought no beer, but found a few bottles in a remote store up the valley, unexpected shoppers as dark closed in. The owner lit a candle for us, and we drank one in his store. He sat opposite and smiled at us, and nodded when we gestured how good it was.

Time passes quickly in such a place. The fishing was good, and we slept well. If we stopped to notice, our guides were less conspicuous than we'd been used to. Kencho was flat-out exhausted each morning, like some kind of alley cat on a mission. Only

Karma joined us for breakfast. By now the drama of his virginity was playing at fever pitch. Karma was fresh out of university, and under pressure he resorted to long, involved accounts of Bhutanese mythology. Though he looked uncannily like James Dean, this just didn't work with the girls. Keen to put an end to the ribbing he was getting, he was taking lessons from whoever would give them. Only Alison was worth listening to: flattery gets you everywhere, she said. Tell them plainly and sincerely that they are beautiful, and the rest will be easy. Karma, habitually, took notes.

We left the Tang, backtracked across the third mountain pass, and south to a hidden valley. Kencho needed the break. He lay flat out in the back seat, groaning over the bumps in the road.

'Hey, Kencho,' said Rod. 'It'll fall off one day.'

The Gangte Chhu lay curled up like a snake on a rock in the hot sun. As we dropped down the hill towards it I saw a sinuous line of reflected light, the river turning in on itself, over and over again. Spring fed, the Gangte seeps out of a valley basin of moss and spongy peat, the water leaching slowly from the upper slopes to the river. Across the marshy plain the Gangte has no idea which way it is heading, but at the end of the valley the gradient picks up and the river straightens out and rushes down across hard rock. Above this sit about six miles of mazy trout stream inside three miles of river valley.

The weather over the Gangte turned a deep blue, muting all the colours in the valley except the bright red spots of the rhododendrons, the same colour as the spots on the trout, and a large sulphur yellow mayfly which shone out of the gloom like a west-coast trawlerman in oilskins.

I sat on the bank at one point to take a picture of Rod and Patrick who stood upstream framed in a symmetry of mist and water. The bank was lined with tussocks of bamboo, and cool water seeped through the bog to trickle down the dark earth into the stream. Strings of bright green algae traced the rivulets. This perfect trout stream had flowed for thousands of years with no trout in it. Until recently, the yellow mayflies could sail downriver without getting eaten.

I caught a trout in a side channel. The water turned through a tunnel of rhododendrons, curled back up the valley, hesitated, turned again, and now in a hurry rattled down through three pools back to the main channel. Briefly, at the tail of the middle pool the water emerged from its tunnel, and in the light the moss grew thick on a shelf of rock which ended the pool. Above this was a perfect lie for a bigger fish.

It was impossible to throw the fly from down-stream without it dragging off the pool. I tried any-way, and saw a flash of light in the water just as my fly pulled a wake in the surface and tumbled over the edge. The second cast I tried from twenty feet back on the bank, side on to the river, my fly line draped over stumps of bamboo and the crimson rhododendron flowers. The trout came again and took the fly. It could have run upstream and broken the line in the tunnel, but the big fish sat in his favourite lie shaking his head until I got above him and dragged him over the rocks. Dark as mahogany, a line of rose spots edged in blue, the gill cover fading to a sort of metallic green, I knew this fish already. I'd caught it at home in Glen Lyon, in the East Lyn. The fish made this strange place familiar.

We caught over forty between us, and the next day even more. The biggest, black and angry, pulled from lairs under crumbling banks and tangles of rhododendrons.

We stayed those last nights in a guesthouse on the edge of the village, the accommodation all on the upper floors above the livestock. The rumour going round at supper was that Karma had negotiated a shared sleeping bag with one of the girls from the kitchen. Later I took a much-needed wash in the bathhouse outside. Lying back with my head on the side of the tub I could see stars through a gap in the roof. Kencho was outside turning rocks on a fire. 'You ready?' he called. 'Let 'em roll,' I said. The rocks cracked and hissed as they hit the water. Moments later vortices of warmth came lapping round me. Steam filled the air. 'Kencho!' I shouted. 'This is fantastic.'

I lay there listening to the dogs. Closer I heard a sharp knocking, then a bang. 'I am not happy.' It was Karma. Kencho started to laugh. 'You idiot,' he said. 'What did you need your toothbrush for?'

'I don't know. I just went to get it. I said I'd be a minute. Now she will not open the door. I've hurt my foot.'

'It's too late.'

Karma limped to the truck in the morning, but wouldn't ride with Ugyen. We all knew Ugyen had been behind the door too. He had no regrets. He was Dr Luurve.

Heaven and Hell on
the Miramichi

'OH MY GOD, WE ARE GOING TO DIE, AND ALL FOR a lousy salmon.'

This guy Steve was tall, bony, angular. He was edgy, but warm too, which was a strange mixture. Willie, our guide, was phlegmatic and quiet. Steve was a bundle of nerves.

A mist enveloped the deep silence over the Cains River. For a moment I could hear the curl of every ripple in the water behind us, and I could hear Steve and Willie breathing. We were all looking at a paw print in the sand – too big to have been made by a dog. A bear had been playing with her cub, and where she had clawed the ground there were deep cuts ten inches long.

'That's a bear all right. Fresh print too. Sand's wet.' Willie turned back to the river. 'The water's come down some since then,' he said, more interested in the meaning of falling water than the presence of a bear. Steve and I stayed where we were, stooped over the print.

'Hell, it could be anywhere,' said Steve. 'It's probably in those bushes there, taking a crap, figuring out which one of us to maul first.'

'I guess we'll have to make a lot of noise on our way back along the trail,' Willie said drily.

This was a high point, for the day had become boring, despite the fiery colours of the forest and the low whisper of running water on its way down to the Miramichi. We weren't catching a thing; we hadn't seen a thing. I worked out that I was casting about eight hundred and forty times in a day, and would have liked at least two of those casts to meet with something – some form of resistance; a pull, or a roll. Even one of the maple leaves, now starting to line the shrinking contours of the water's edge, would have made my heart miss a beat if it had brushed past my line. But sixteen hundred and eighty casts had met nothing at all. I could hear Steve's line moving through the damp air; a rhythmic swish that seemed absurdly geometric in the face of the random wildness we were trying to capture. He was working his way down the pool for the third time, while I sat on the grass hoping a bear would turn up. The end of the second day.

Optimism is the caffeine of Atlantic salmon fishing. I inject it over twelve or twenty-four months, trying to forget the last trip, or reducing the memory until only the tension remains. And so each time I arrive full of hope. I hit Fredericton as the sun came low over the trees and the river. A copper glow played on the colonnades and porches. I drove along the waterfront, through the town centre, past its ornate buildings, theatres with Doric columns, grass and clean pavements, and then out north into the darkening country where the road rolled up and down like a deep, mid-sea swell; a ribbon of black, hard ocean running between trees, their autumn colours muted by this slow dusk.

I was looking for signs to the Miramichi. On the radio the DJ was talking to a local teacher.

'So the school burnt down?'

'Yes, and now all the classes are in the fire station, or church,' the teacher explained cheerfully. 'The community is pulling together.'

'And I see here, you were out, er . . . moose hunting when the fire broke out?' It wasn't obvious from the tone whether hunting moose while your school burns was a good thing to do or a sign of negligence.

The road seemed endless, as unfamiliar roads do, and apart from the swell, everything was flat. In the fading light I noticed road signs every mile or so, with pictures of salmon, as if you had to be careful not to hit one crossing the road. When I stopped at a garage to ask directions, they knew right away where Wade's camp was. In the rack I noticed two rows of books on salmon fishing sandwiched between bridal manuals and needlework instruction.

My notes told me the camp was dry, suggesting

that guests bring along whatever drink they prefer. I asked where the beer was kept. A girl mopping the floor stood aside, pointing to the back corner of the store at a walk-in fridge the size of a cattle truck, stacked high with cans. She closed the door behind me. I paid over a counter inside the fridge, and only then was I let out again: you'd have to suffer a lot of hit-and-run beer raids to bring on this level of security. The cash till seemed unguarded.

Outside huge trucks hissed past on the black, damp tarmac, and then some distance away the hiss turned into a hollow rumble, as though they were crossing a bridge. I wanted to go and look at the river I'd travelled so far to fish, but it was too late and too dark. I took the turning I was told to, dodging pot-holes along a back road through thick forest until I reached a clearing in the pine trees.

In the weak light I saw a cluster of huts of different sizes. I wandered about in the dark, opening doors and calling out. The huts all had front porches enclosed with mosquito netting, their doors on those creaky springs that shut behind you with a thin bang – the noise recalls boss-eyed, trailer-park psychos in dirty vests and no trousers, who lean on the door pillar and eat beans out of a tin can with their hands. The office lights were on, and the same radio programme I'd been listening to in the car was playing – 'Mary Lou says hi to Juicy Luke, says she misses him, wants him home soon.' But I found no party of drunk fishermen huddled round a fly-tying vice, and no one to tell me how the river was fishing.

At last George, the manager, found me by my car and told me everyone was asleep. He showed me to my room, told me that the Miramichi flowed right past the window, checked the hot water, and went to bed himself. It was about ten o'clock. I couldn't sleep, I sat on the porch listening to the river.

In the morning I drew back the curtain and saw it. The Miramichi. Early mist hung just above the surface, softening the reflected colours of the far bank. George, dressed in trainers and tracksuit pants, came up the steps from the boat ramp, turned at the top, and walked down them again. I counted him up and down five times, before I stepped on to the porch. I could hear him panting and his steps getting louder.

'Hiya,' said George, next time up. He was sweating wildly. 'Morning exercise. Trying to get in shape.'

'Good for you.'

'You're to fish with Willie. That's him over there. Steve's with him already.' He pointed to someone sitting on rocks on the far side of the river. 'Hey Willie!' George shouted, and beckoned Willie over. He turned back to me. 'Get your stuff and get over there.'

'Time for a coffee?'

'If you hurry. He's on his way now.'

Willie jumped into his boat and pulled at the motor cord. I fetched a rod, and watched his boat split the flat surface of the water.

This was 'The Run', an unprepossessing, but apparently famous, stretch of water at the top end of the camp beat. Steve, already hip deep, gave a wave from the far side. A little way up from him were four more anglers in a row, opposite them another three.

'Who are those guys?' I nodded upriver on the way over.

'Mostly retired doctors,' said Willie. 'The Blackbrook Club.'

'The Blackbrook Club? Sounds like some gang of preppy New Yorkers.'

'They only fish 'bout three hundred yards of bank.' He paused. 'That's some three hundred yards, though.'

I looked upriver. It seemed the same as the bit in front of me. Twenty minutes later, I heard a yip, and watched one of them land a salmon. An hour passed and that happened again. The river was high, and dirty after rain. Our sport was slow. Steve worked down ahead of me for fifty yards, waded out, sat on the bank for a few minutes chatting to Willie, then got in upstream again. I did the same. We rotated perhaps six times during the morning. A few fish rolled, or lazily belly-flopped on the flat surface, as if to show you they were there. Two more salmon came off the Blackbrook water before we crossed the stream for lunch. Then I looked upriver as some elderly gent landed a fourth. He saw me and waved. I waved back. He shouted something but I couldn't hear him.

Back at camp we talked about whether the river was rising or falling, clearing or colouring. Two other guys who'd been fishing downriver asked us hopefully what we thought the prospects were, looking for an opinion more expert than their own. Steve shrugged, and looked at me. I said I'd never fished for salmon in Canada, and that I was hoping one of them would know. We looked out the window at the edge of the stream. One of the guys said that it looked a little lower than earlier. 'A good sign, at least,' I said. 'Is it?' he asked. He paused for a moment, then added brightly, 'Yes, you're right, it is.' He hurried down to the edge of the water, built a pile of stones, and put a stick in the mud. We watched the stick and the stones during lunch. If the river moved, it didn't move much. At last someone said that a record number of fish had swum past the counter that year.

'Well, let's go catch some of them,' said Steve, standing up.

But the afternoon was dead. I took some pictures of Steve deep in the Miramichi, the river a flat mirror of the dark shades of the forest. I needed a picture of a fish, though. No fish, no story. I promised my wife I'd call, and packed up a few minutes early to get back to the camp, thinking I wouldn't miss much. When Steve showed up for supper he told me he'd caught a small salmon, just after I left. 'Well there you go,' I said. 'Wouldn't have even seen it if I'd stayed. What did you take it on?' 'A Black Bear with a green butt.' The next day, back at the same place I knew which fly Steve was going to use. When a fish moved in front of George, a new face who was fishing with us, he called over to Steve: 'Hey, have you got another Black Bear with a green butt?' These are the little coat-pegs we hang our Atlantic salmon hopes on. Earlier we'd talked of fly patterns, and Steve, a computer programmer, shrugged his shoulders and said, 'Well they'll say such and such a fly takes 80 per cent of the fish, but if 80 per cent of the fishermen are using it, what d'ya expect?' This is a truth we all know, though we ignore it all the time. 'Last year I caught all mine on a Blue Charm,' he added after a pause.

Not even the Black Bear worked that morning.

As we packed up for lunch Steve sighed, 'Well we tried.' Then added, 'The water's come down some, though. I'm sure it has. Later that gravel bar will be out – then we'll kill 'em.'

At lunch the mood lifted. We had experts at the table. Two new guys had shown up, and already one of them, Bruce, had caught a salmon. Bruce had fair hair, and a voice so deep that everything he said had the pitch of a film-trailer voiceover. The salt cellar moved when he spoke. His buddy, John, was a whirl-wind. He chewed quickly, and didn't stop chewing to make fast, professional announcements on the state of the river, and salmon fishing in general. He was witty and intense – a big hitter in publishing.

The dynamics of the group changed subtly and instinctively – these guys had caught a fish within hours of arriving. 'A Green Machine was getting all the attention,' said Bruce. I asked John how much was the fly and how much the place, wondering why I was always in the wrong place.

'Bottom line,' said John as he put a forkful of potato and ham into his mouth, 'it's the law of numbers. The longer your fly is in the water, the greater your chance of catching a fish. Then he added, staring straight ahead into the fireplace, 'But man, when they go, those fish'll tear you a new asshole.' He shook his head, and stuck his fork into another potato, as though somehow what he had said was literally true, and something ought to be done about it.

The television was on quietly in the corner, news-casters miming words to pictures of destruction and mayhem. Hurricane George was the big story, and one of the rods was worried about his house.

'Leave that on, willya?' he said, 'I just want to check if it's headed to my house. Well, the one where I spend the winter, in Florida. Naples.' I guessed from his tone that we were supposed to be impressed. But I'd never heard of Naples in Florida, so the mean-ing was lost on me, and the other lunchers had started to drift away.

The afternoon was another long slog. I fished hard for five hours without a touch, as did Steve and George. We were on new water, so we started with an intensity that new water can bring on. But it dies away after a while. Willie watched us from the bank in that way a headmaster watches the playground at break time, and I felt morally obliged to keep going, even though I had been overtaken by a sense of futility. I knew the feeling well. It replaces the optimism. A fish crashed downriver at the end of the pool. 'Hear that,' shouted Steve. 'That's the sound of destiny. My destiny. That fish is coming upriver, and I'm gonna catch it.' Later that afternoon we found the bear print.

In the evening we discovered that Bruce had caught another two, including a fish of twenty-four pounds. I needed a picture of a fish. At least if I witnessed the capture of one of these mythical beasts I'd have my story. 'Steve,' I said. 'Do me a favour and catch one too, will you?' 'I'm trying,' said Steve. 'I'm trying.' Bruce accepted our weak congratulations with a convincing but practised modesty. He said it was just being in the right place at the right time. A euphemism for knowing what you're doing.

Throughout supper we spoke about what flies to use. John had seen some fish caught at the Blackbrook, on a pattern he said looked like a bear turd. He tied some up. 'What's it called?' asked George. 'The Bear Turd,' said John. Bruce had been catching all his fish on his Green Machine – a cigar tied with deer hair that looked like a green bear turd. John's fly got smashed to pieces by several fish in the afternoon, though he didn't catch one. He left supper early to tie some more. 'John doesn't really come here to relax,' said Bruce. He then quickly stood up and went off to tie some of his own.

The evening died away almost before it began. These two whirlwind fishers had brought a sense of urgent professionalism to the camp. Soon there was just me and Steve, the TV and the guy with the house in Florida, who was worrying again, and just wanted to make sure the storm wasn't headed to where he spent the winter, in Florida, at Naples. I checked Steve's face. It betrayed no emotion at the mention of Naples.

I needed a picture of a salmon.

The next morning after breakfast I left to travel upstream. I was due to fish a different camp for a couple of days, and as I started the car the first spits of rain began to kick up dust and pine needles out in front of the dining room. The rain hardened until it was bouncing off the windscreen, and sheets of water slewed across the road.

Wilson's camp was further upstream. By the time I got there the river was rising. I was directed towards a track up the valley, which turned down alongside the river. Up from here a gravel shallow faded into the dark mist. The river seemed more approachable than at Wade's, of a scale that could be understood and analysed. This didn't make me feel any better. I stood there, rain dripping off the rim of my hat, watching an angler and guide work down the pool. The futility of their endeavour overwhelmed me. I recognised this too, as a moment which occurs more or less whenever I fish for salmon. Letting go of hope. Like Rutger Hauer's android in *Blade Runner*,

I see intergalactic cities aflame. I touch the brutal absurdity of the universe. I wake up and discover I am a beetle. The guide waved and waded over. 'Hi, I'm Tyler,' he said when he reached me. I shook his hand. 'We'll let Max finish that run there, then have lunch on the porch of our cabin. Go wait up there if you like.'

'Fishing any good?' I asked. I knew the answer.

Tyler breathed in. 'Slow,' he said. 'But there's the afternoon. There are fish in there all right. Just a matter of gettin' one to take.'

'River's rising too. That won't help.'

'Well, I've sure caught one or two salmon on a rising river.'

'Perhaps,' I said. 'But not today. I don't need the remote possibility of catching something, I need the likelihood. I need a salmon to save my soul.'

'Well, Charles,' said Tyler. 'You won't catch one unless your line's in the water.'

A good point, but not a good start. The moaning Brit. Tyler wasn't impressed. He was too polite to show it. Max came in for lunch. Cam and Chick joined us from upriver. They took the slow sport with better grace than I did. For them it was all part of salmon fishing.

'Hey,' said Cam. 'You want certainty, go to a fish farm.' Another good point.

'Yes, yes. You're right, I know. But sometimes with these salmon, you have got to wonder what the hell you're playing at.'

'That's the whole point. I like to wonder what I'm playing at.'

We had lunch on the porch of the cabin overlooking the river, and listened to rain drum on the roof. A veil of fog followed the curves of the river, and either side the copper and yellow of autumn broke through, and receded, until the trees also faded from sight into a blue distance.

Some time during one of my days up there a fish pulled my fly. When sport is slow the normally cynical guides will seize on a mini-event like this and wrap all the hope in the universe around it. I called downstream that I had a pull on the fly. Tyler left Max, and came walking up to me.

'Did you have a take, Charles?'

Now I wasn't so sure. It could have been anything. I looked at the water. It could have been the rock midstream, or the pull of current on the line, the fly bumping a log.

'Don't know. Maybe. I can't be sure. I mean there was a pull, but I can't say it was a fish.'

'It probably was. They're in here all right, and that's a good spot.'

'Yeah, but it could have been a rock.'

'That was a fish, Charles, I'd say. Fish that spot again. Go through real careful. Maybe change the fly a couple of times.'

I did as he said, paced up the bank three times and came down on that spot each go with a new fly.

I didn't get the pull again, so it might not have been a rock, but that didn't make it a fish. It could have been a leaf. By the time I got back to camp and sat down for supper I had apparently played a big fish for some time.

At lunch on the last day we joined Cam and Chick by the river. Cam was smiling furtively.

'What's up?' I asked. 'You've caught one, haven't you?'

'Caught a salmon,' said Cam, nodding his head.

'How big?' I asked.

Cam didn't answer. He just stood there, looking at me with this grin on his face.

'About thirty-two pounds,' said Chick.

'You know,' said Cam. 'They say every once in a while a blind hog will bump into an acorn. I think I just bumped into mine.'

'I can't believe it,' I said. 'That's huge. Thirty-two pounds? Fantastic. Well done. Thirty-two pounds. Some salmon.' Suddenly I remembered my photo. 'Oh my God. You should have called us on the radio. I need a picture. I need a picture of one of these creatures.'

After lunch their guide played a tape on their truck radio he thought I might find funny. It was the Miramichi river guide song, called 'You should have been here last week'. How I laughed.

I didn't catch a fish until the last day, until I'd given up all thought of catching one. I was back at Wade's.

Steve and I fished the home pool. A thin grey mist lay across the river and the trees rose up into it, their tops invisible. Upstream the Blackbrook Club were already lining their hallowed yards of river bank. You could hear every word, wafting downstream in the soft air. Every so often there'd be a whoop and a splash, and 'Hey, way to go. What d'ya take him on?' Up there in the mist they seemed to occupy another celestial level, and down here we could only catch glimpses and fragments of sound that let us know what it was like in Miramichi heaven.

Steve was clapping his hands in readiness for an exciting morning. Some of his excitement was manufactured to help overcome the likelihood of another three hours of fruitless casting, and some was real because on a new day you never know.

Then I caught a grilse, as though it was the easiest thing. The fish came out of nowhere, intersecting the five-thousandth cast I'd put across the Miramichi, like I was some milestone customer in a used car lot. I had my picture. Steve looked happy for me, though his casting was a little sharper for a while afterwards. I relaxed and caught a salmon. This time Steve strained out a plea.

'Oh God. Oh God. There's got to be one salmon in here with faulty vision, or one called Crazy Louie. Yeah they all say, that Crazy Louie, he'll bite at anything.'

Steve still had too much hope in his soul.

Ain't Got Deet, Ain't Got Shit

THE HOTEL DINING ROOM IN KUUJJUAQ HAS LARGE windows that look out over the town. I could see down the length of the main dirt road and into the back yards of the painted wooden houses – bright toys strewn across a patch of hard ground; a shirt and jeans drying in the wind; three quad bikes parked by a back porch, one in pieces. Beyond lay a grey stage of ocean.

'I prefer the Twin Otter any day. More power, more load capacity. She won't let you down.'

'OK, those are points, but to get you in *and* out of a hole, you gotta go Single Otter. Man, 'gainst a headwind that pup will lift you inside a hunna feet. 'Gainst a wind she's like a goddam helicopter.'

'He's gotta point.'

'Twin'll get you into a place with 'nuff stuff that you won't have to get out in such a goddam hurry, you ask me. 'Sall I'm saying.'

The talk tailed off for a few seconds. Here was

my chance to say something, but I didn't know what it should be, so I continued with my ham and chips, looking out the window. Four guys – Steve A, Steve M, Kregg and Cliff – were arguing about which kind of plane was best in the northern wilderness.

As they talked on I thought of a question.

'Which one are we going in this afternoon?'

'Twin, ain't it?' said Cliff looking at Steve A, who nodded. Cliff folded his arms.

'So, it's a Twin,' said Kregg. 'That's OK by me. Doesn't mean it's a better plane.'

Steve A was guiding us up the Ungava peninsula to the Payne River, the first week in the season, just after ice-out. Kuujjuaq, a town on the very edge of the tree line, was only the half-way point, and north of it lay mile after mile of empty, monotonous land broken only by rivers and lakes. Kregg and Cliff ran outdoor goods stores in California. Steve M made videos which he sold to cable TV. 'Hi, I'm Steve,' he said to me back where we started in Montreal. 'I'm Mr Lake Trout. What I don't know about lake trout is not worth knowing.'

'There lake trout up there, then?'

'Lakers *and* sea-run char. But the lakers are not your fat, lazy fellas from some places. These boys *fight*.' Steve talked as though the camera was always rolling.

In the hut at Kuujjuaq airfield, we stood around fidgeting, kicking the soft-drink dispenser, going to the pissoir in rotation. I read the notices: a canoe race in Kuujjuaq to celebrate Canada Day, and afterwards a five buck bar-b-q with bring your own beer; the single mums' book club meets every Thursday, 7 p.m., Town Hall, this week's book *Paris Trout*; depression counselling is available the same time on a Friday. One of the guys went outside for a smoke. I followed him out to get a look at the country. Beyond the oil-stained dust of the paddock and the fuel silos, two planes on deflated tyres oxidised at the scrub edge. The guy ahead of me lit up. He waved the air above his face, threw his smoke on to the ground and ran back into the foyer.

'Fuckin' mossies,' he said as he passed.

Suddenly one was up my nose, another in my ear.

Kregg and Cliff laughed when I got back inside.

'Somethin', in't they?' said Kregg, chuckling so that his heavy shoulders shook.

'Those things are evil,' I said.

'Better believe it.' Kregg had seen it all before. He had marked me down as the soft Englishman.

I searched my bag. Kregg looked on. He nodded at Cliff and jerked his thumb at me.

'What's that girly smell?' asked Kregg.

'Repellant,' I answered.

'Smells like goddam perfume.'

'That stuff won't do nuthin',' added Cliff, nodding his chin at it. 'Up here, you ain't got Deet, you ain't got shit.'

Our plane bucked in the updraughts, running under a ceiling of low cloud. The land unrolled beneath us, a bare expanse of water and bog, the water like pieces in a jigsaw, spread out over the floor. In the hollows and on the northern slopes, patches of snow stood out against the slate green of a landscape that was only just waking up.

We flew over a herd of caribou, the animals scattering at the noise of our aircraft, splashing through the river beneath us. Looking up from the herd, towards the hill from which they walked, and beyond, it became clear that caribou stretched to the horizon, coalescing in the distance to one amorphous, migratory mass. We were all distracted by the sight, including the pilot. He suddenly banked the plane upwards. We hit the ground with a crash that echoed through the fuselage and set the altimeter shrieking. The plane bounced twice before it slowed. When we stopped, the pilot took off his earphones and turned round.

'Sorry, guys. That is the worst landing I've ever done. Definitely the worst.'

I unpeeled my hands from the frame of the seat in front of me. Everyone had a hold of something, and a nervous laugh rippled through the plane. I said to the guy in front, 'If there's a line between landing and crashing we were on it.'

'A landing is just a controlled collision,' said one of the Otter experts.

'Besides, you bring one of these things down so hard you'll spit fillings, the plane'll be just fine.'

I'd seen him hold on just as tight as I had.

Caribou moved like a river round the cobble strip that we'd landed on. Over a mile away, on the far side of the estuary we'd come to fish, lines of the animals tracked over the ridge, down to the water. A few were swimming across towards our shore.

'Millions of them,' said Steve A. 'I've never seen a herd like this.'

They passed our camp for three days without a break, so many that the high-water mark along the estuary was covered by a dark line of caribou hair.

It's hard to travel so far and still have to wait to go fishing, but the tide was on the way out, leaving behind it a shelf of drying stone. Boulders stood like gravestones above the cobble bed. Soon the sea was far away beyond the rocks.

I walked to the high-water mark. A fishing party who had beaten the tide were unloading their catch. The guide cleaned their fish at a table awash with dark blood and against it the sparkle of fish scales and fat sea-run char, silver and green in the light, split open to reveal crimson flesh. Beside them was a pile of pan-sized brook trout, green with red spots, and also lake trout, as long as my leg, camouflaged like tanks. The guide wore a yellow oilskin, and his tough hands worked quickly. A cigarette hung from his mouth, and he looked up to smile and nod. 'Some fish,' I said. He packed the fish carefully into a box, wiped his knife on a cloth, and threw a bucket of sea water over the table. Dilute red flowed like a watershed in miniature to gather in a pool on the edge of the estuary, and I stood hypnotised by this river within a river. I looked out over the wasteland of stone and tidal pools and felt like I'd crossed space. I left the guide to finish his work, and went to find which cabin I'd been allotted.

'You pick that one or that one. These ones is already picked,' said Kregg.

Each of the taken beds had a baseball cap on the pillow. Two other beds framed the propane stove we'd use to heat our wooden hut. I picked the one nearest a small window, thinking that in such tight quarters farts might be an issue.

Kregg was by his bed unloading gear from a cavernous holdall.

'Always pick the bed by the door,' he said. 'It can get a little muggy in a room this size.'

'I suppose so, though you'll get eaten first by curious bears.'

'Bears won't come in here if you don't keep food in here,' he said seriously. 'You bothered by snoring, by the way? 'Cos if you are you might want to fetch some ear-plugs. Cliff snores some. I know, I've shared with him before.'

Cliff appeared at the door, filling the frame. He wore a white T-shirt stretched tight over his belly, camo trousers and fourteen-eye boots.

'Oh no, you don't mind snoring, do you?'

'Well, no. Depends how loud.'

'Oh, it's loud,' said Kregg. 'Hell, I'm used to it. I

wake up when he stops. I think he might be dead or something.'

'It'll be fine,' I said.

It wasn't. Cliff snored like a diesel goods train climbing a hill.

Steve C, a Montana writer and my boat partner for the week, arrived on the next afternoon. I was taking a nap in the cabin. Steve noticed Cliff's alarm clock on the shelf, picked it up and held it to his ear.

'Oh shit,' he said. 'He's got a ticking clock. That'll have to go under a pillow.'

'You might think that the ticking would keep you awake,' I said. 'But it won't.'

'How's that?'

'You won't hear it above the snoring.'

Dawn the next morning Steve woke saying, 'You didn't keep me awake at all, I just dreamt of crashing cars, intense bombardments, that kind of thing.' He turned to look at me, and mimed an expression of intense terror. Cliff smiled. 'I'll find you guys some ear-plugs,' he said.

Junesie Kudluk was our guide. He waited for us in his freighter canoe while we bolted a coffee in the dining hut, then took us to the base of a small island in the middle of the estuary, threw his anchor overboard, and gestured for us to start. It was first thing in the morning, high tide, and the early light – up here it never got truly dark – was brightening the slate grey rocks and the white patches of ice on the far side of the estuary. The high mottled cloud pattern drew a vanishing point in the sky, like nebulous graph paper curling down to the horizon, and strangely, an icing of low cloud never lifted off the cold rocks that surrounded us. Junesie told us that the island was haunted, that long ago a mother abandoned her baby there, and that the sea drowned this woman because she was wicked.

Apart from this, Junesie said little. His English was poor – our Inuktitut worse – though he knew important stuff like 'here big fish', or 'over there, better.' It was difficult to tell what animated him, but he liked to reach the fishing grounds before the others. Sometimes he gave everyone a head start. A slight smile would crack the edges of his leathery face, straighten his incongruously dictatorial moustache, as his boat drew alongside and then away from the rest – though he never looked round. He'd done something to his outboard.

My fly rod buckled aggressively, and the spinning reel-handle caught my knuckle. My first strike on only the third cast: something had hit the fly on the run. Holding the rod high I reached for the hub of the reel with my left hand to turn the drag up and slow the running fish. It leapt through the surface thirty yards off the stern, a bright char, over two feet long. It spun and pulled, cutting angles across the surface. As the fish tired the angles became shorter, until at the edge of the boat it thumped feebly against the rod. I bent down to run my hand along its emerald flank towards the mouth, where I turned out the hook as the fish lay on its side in the water, the most colourful thing in a drab landscape.

'You'll fly across the world for that,' I said to Steve, happy now that I had caught my fish, felt through it this new place.

Later Steve hooked into a fish that ran and ran. The reel didn't stop or slow until the line neared the hub of the spool, and Steve had to clamp hard to break the tippet rather than lose everything. We never saw the fish, just heard the singing reel, the crack of the nylon. Not long after that he boated a fish the size of a small dog. He held it for a picture, grimacing against the stinging rain that was passing over just then. That fish had a jaw that could have swallowed a child. I looked down into the billowing clouds of kelp, astonished at the richness of a food chain that could create these creatures. Sea-run char feed for only a few months in salt water, but they pack on weight by murdering capelin and shrimp.

It's wrong to become complacent about wild fish but after a while we stopped doubting that we would catch them. There was no feeling that the moment would pass. Instead we started looking for the fifteen-pounders we'd been told about. Four-pound char went back with a comment about how pretty they are. This didn't surprise me, though I had never known anything like it. Fishermen need to look for the difficult or evasive, redefining the context to accommodate whatever that may be; thus fish get measured all ways, not just in inches. Here though, there was little else; the prize was for the biggest.

We caught fewer with a fly than did the others – all of whom were spin-fishers – but even so Steve and I boated more fish than seemed decent to count, and we lost track of numbers. This irked and puzzled Kregg and Cliff who every so often would call over, 'How many you got?'

'Dunno,' we'd call back, 'maybe twenty.'

'Uh huh. I got fort'two, Cliff's got thirt'eight. Oh hold up, he's got thirt'nine now.'

We'd see Cliff's broad shoulders hunch down, his arm swipe sideways, then lift, another char thrashing on the end of a line. Kregg would crank his bait a little faster while watching Cliff's fish, and if they got two on at once Kregg would cackle with the satisfaction of it. They fished in full camouflage, though we were in boats in the Arctic tundra, the nearest mottled vegetation several hundred miles to the south.

In turn, I suppose that Kregg and Cliff regarded us two writers, writers who insisted on fly-fishing, with some degree of suspicion. Me especially, a Brit with a wax jacket. Steve C, who after all did own a pair of camo trousers, cut the ice better than I did.

The estuary changed shape imperceptibly as we fished through the day. For hours it seemed to lie idle, a vast unchanging lake. A burst of sun drew my attention away from the water, and the endless run of fish, to notice that the lake had shrunk, that a line of spray blowing on the wind below us marked a waterfall we'd motored right over when the tide was full. We ran it now with Junesie picking a path between boulders as big as trucks.

A group of anglers was already ashore, their boats moored along a spine of rocks. The guides cleaned fillets of char at the water's edge. Shortly the whole party had arrived, coffee was steaming over a fire, and the smell of frying onions and fresh fish reminded us all that it had been many hours since breakfast.

Steve M was standing with a plate ready for the first chunk of fish that came off the pan.

'For me the Arctic char is tops in the fish world. Nothing tastes better.' He grinned, and held. But his cameraman had missed it, flat out on the rocks, sunning himself despite the chill wind. Steve C and I fetched coffee, and sat down to watch the camo twins fish off the stern of their moored boat while they waited for their fillets to cook. Every so often one would hook into a fish, and Kregg would chuckle and say, 'Fift'faw,' then later 'Fift'five'.

'Hey, guys, why you counting?' Steve called over. 'Isn't it good enough to say "a lot"?'

'Thing is,' said Cliff, ''less we count no one will believe us.'

'You gotta put an exact number on,' Kregg joined in. 'A lot can mean anything to any number of people. We're recording how many and the biggest.'

Steve M sat down near us, his plate piled high with fillets and onions.

'You guys fly-fishing, aren't you? How you getting along?'

'We're doing well.'

'Getting down deep enough? I'll tell ya,' he said, pulling out a strange lure – a lead ball wrapped in latex, it looked like something the French would give you to treat piles – 'this is the hot plug. Not because of the pattern, but because of where it's fishing . . . *on the bottom*.'

'We're getting them up top,' I said.

I lay on my bed that evening listening to Steve C chatting about camo with the camo twins, while I played with Kregg's new GPS device, trying to work out how far I was from home.

'Which is selling for you guys?' asked Steve.

'It's a fashion thing,' said Cliff.

Kregg nodded. 'Right now folks are going for the chaparral look – say Shadowgrass. Last year though we killed 'em with lines in Advantage Wetlands and Break-Up.'

'Yeah,' said Steve. 'And I've seen a lot of guys getting into that Diamondback line.'

'That's good,' agreed Cliff. 'A bit gimmicky, but it works.'

'Uh huh. Counters that blobbiness at distance? Kind of diffuse? That the idea?'

'Yup.'

'OK. Earth calling,' I interrupted. 'I can't believe

you have fashion lines in camouflage. Are you serious?'

'For sure. Some folk wear camo pyjamas.'

I gave up with the GPS machine – I couldn't work it anyhow; I just knew I was a long way away.

We woke particularly early one morning to run the Payne River inland, as far as we could get in two hours aboard Junesie's tweaked canoe. Lines of migrating caribou split the hillsides, running like paint from up high to the water's edge, and we couldn't help but pass through flotillas of them swimming from one shore to the other. Eyes wide they'd churn in the water, not knowing which way to turn, until we passed, when they resumed their passage: the same as when you run your finger through the scent of an ant trail, and for a few moments they bounce around like pin-balls trying to find the right way.

Further in we began to ascend. Junesie was a good boatman, and made easy work of the vast river, which slid down towards us with the dangerous power of lava flow. Half-way up one long rapid Junesie pulled hard over and rested the boat. In a tight gap in the rocks the water spun like a typhoon. He nodded at the dark pool. I stood and cast. The white streamer dropped through peaty water, and a fish rose from the bottom of the river to meet it, opened its mouth, swallowed the fly and turned down, a slow easy movement. Even when I struck the lake trout hardly changed his course, instead swimming only with a degree more deliberate power for the bottom of the river. He weighed seven pounds, had a head like a pit-bull terrier.

Above here the gradient eased off, and the pools stretched away to the horizon, linked together by a chain of snaking rapids. Steve C stepped out of the boat at one, on to a gravel shoal, and taking his lighter fly rod began to cast for brook trout in the foamy water below. One slammed the streamer fly first cast, and as Steve brought the fish in a lake trout turned at it. When hooked, the brook trout become live bait: the prey of vast lakers which cruise the rock shelves. Sometimes we would bring back a mauled and crippled fish.

Steve A caught a big laker, and held it for a picture – its belly sagged with weight, its head and shoulders were heavy and rounded. It had a dumb, podgy face and reminded me of a prize-fighter, not menacing, but scary for being bullishly strong, with no sense of when to stop.

Further up the river we passed a derelict Inuit village sited on an island of green pasture, and beyond that a cluster of corrugated huts by the river, used as an overnight station by fishermen, only once or twice each year. Inside one we found a kettle, some dry sticks for a fire. We brewed up by the river, and watched the caribou herd, still passing, press on up the valley. One of the cabin doors had been peeled open at its top edge, and claw marks scarred the corrugated roof.

'Some bear's gotta sniff of food in there,' said Cliff. 'Reckon we'll have to lock up careful tonight.'

'You staying up here?' asked Steve C, sounding hopeful.

'Sure,' said Kregg. 'We're gonna stay up, fish the evening, and fix to get a big one of these lakers.'

'Make our way down in the mornin', catch the estuary tide, and see you guys back home tomorrow night. We're on nearly a hunnad a day at the moment. Reckon if we get tomorrow right we can top a hunnad, and catch three different types of fish.'

'I felt I'd like to join them,' I said to Steve as we pulled off into the pool, heading downriver, 'but for the prospect of a night without snoring.'

'Don't even think about it. You'll be tortured by snoring then mauled by a bear.'

On the way back we picked up a caribou skull. We'd seen it on the way up, a clean skull with huge antlers, resting on the shoreline. It was mossy and damp and smelt of putrefaction and I'd refused to share a boat with it for a day, in spite of how good it would look on Steve's barn or Harley-Davidson, or wherever he wanted to put it. After some anxious searching we found it three feet under water – the tide had covered it, and Steve netted it into the boat. Its green ooze spilt out over the deck.

'How the hell are you going to get that back to Montana?'

'In a bag,' said Steve, as though I'd asked the stupidest question.

Junesie was poker faced – he'd seen it all before. I changed the subject. 'That number thing the camos have got going is funny, don't you think? I hate the idea of counting, and I think to myself, shit they're not even fly-fishing, but then I also find myself thinking, well that's the twenty-second today, and it's bigger than anything they've got.'

'Face it, Charles,' said Steve. 'You want to whup their redneck asses.'

The estuary was quieter without Kregg and Cliff. Their enthusiasm had fed the rest of us and now, in their absence, we missed it. These char were so abundant, so easy to catch. The camo twins, though, never tired. 'We need to cut this up a bit, Steve,' I said midway through the morning. 'Go fish off the rocks, or something. I never thought catching so many fish could become dull.'

Junesie took us to a reef of rocks exposed by the low tide, and we got out of the boat and walked. Here the current heaved and ripped as it passed over and around the rocks – more like a river than the monotonous depths of the main estuary. A boat can become claustrophobic, and I was happier feeling the rocks under my feet, able to move. Out of curiosity I chose a deer-hair mouse pattern.

'Hey Steve, watch this! Squeak, squeak, squeak.'

I pulled the mouse in short, urgent bursts. It chopped a wake across the water, ducking under, bobbing to the top, its leather tail wiggling with each pull. Bow waves appeared left and right, chasing down the mouse until it vanished into a spiralling hole in the water. Line ripped off the fly reel, pulsing on and on. Finally it slowed and stopped, and a long way out across the water a big fish rolled its head violently at the surface.

'Holy smoke. Did you see that?'

'Yeah sure,' said Steve. 'Got any more of those mice?'

Steve and I fished happily across the ebbing tide. At times three, four, even five fish would rush at the lure, cutting trails across the surface towards it, meeting in a violent boil of sharp waves. Then the rod would come alive, and the reel would shriek as the line rushed out. Other boats joined us on the rocks. The guides stood around talking quietly, while we whooped and yeehawed at fish. I noticed we were backing higher up the rocks, away from the reef, and as the strong current slackened, our sport slowed also. It became bright and still. We sat on the rocks, flicking stones and staring abstractedly into the water.

'What the hell is that?'

Steve spotted the whales first: three white vaporous shapes broken by ripples and reflections. They moved quickly, coursing around our headland and into the bay. Junesie and the other guides, Johnny and Noah, had been sitting together, smoking and talking some distance from us along the rocks. Suddenly they were on their feet, urgently running, shouting. Noah stepped on my fly rod as he ran past along the shoreline keeping pace with the whales. He smashed the tip, but didn't stop. Johnny and Junesie ran to their boats, threw fishing tackle out of the way on to the shore, lifted boards. Junesie was at the back of his boat pulling at the starter cord. Johnny jumped in holding a rusted .303 rifle. The boat barked into life and quickly cut across the bay, following the instructions of Noah on the shore. When the smallest whale broke the surface Johnny shot it twice, and the noise echoed across the bay. The whale dropped under the surface, as thin streaks of blood traced through the water.

'Shit,' someone called. 'Watch out for ricochets.'

Johnny was tracking the whale back towards us. It would surface again any moment. We'd sat somewhat paralysed by the intensity of the hunt, but suddenly we scrambled for cover, ducking down behind a narrow ledge as two more shots cracked the air like a whip.

The whale slowed now, Johnny dropped his rifle and the next time it surfaced he sunk a harpoon deep into its rubbery flesh. Blood billowed into the clear water, until the bay was pink with it.

Johnny fastened a rope around its tail, slid the knot tight, and Junesie motored for a gap in the rocks. They hauled the whale up by its tail, across a sloping rock, and butchered it to the bone. All the while they talked excitedly, and chewed on pieces of the rubbery flesh, a delicacy which they offered round to the rest of us.

'Don't touch it,' said Steve. 'It'll give you the runs.'

'This is our first beluga this year,' said Johnny. 'It has been a bad year. Until now nothing, so this is very good.'

Junesie carried his quarter away, and smiled warmly at us as we stood by. In the hunting of this whale, in the way in which, for thirty minutes, our expensive fishing tackle was an inconvenience and we didn't exist, our place here was firmly defined: lucky guests. Noah came up to me to apologise for breaking my fly rod. I told him to forget it. I have a friend at the makers who just loves to talk about warranties. This excuse would get pinned to the wall in the foyer.

I wanted a second chance: to catch all of those char again, and to appreciate them better. To the Inuit the char were fish to be eaten. All week I'd felt that Junesie could only understand the few fish which we caught before lunch, to kill and eat. The others that went back – he had no idea why we fished for them at all.

The camo twins appeared out of an evening mist later that day, Kregg standing at the head of the boat. The tide was running out, and their boat scraped the bottom.

'How'd ya get on?' I asked.

'We got us a lot of fish,' Kregg called out. 'Some big ones too. Cliff got a hunnad and eight and I had a hunnad and twelve. How about you guys?'

'Oh. We had a few,' said Steve.

Ennui

TO GET IT STARTED I HAD TO PADDLE THE THING down the road like I was a flatulent duck. But there's a slight incline from Jim's café across the junction, straight at the river. The timing had to be good or I'd drown. My sandwiches, tackle belt and waders slung into the saddle-bags, my rod strung under the crossbar, and keyed up on Jim's strong coffee I hit the road, heading downstream. The air on the ride down smelt of woodsmoke, and under the avenues of trees, in corners the sun had not yet reached, it was rich and musty. I caught the scents of apples, chickens, drying maize. Already farmers and their families were in the fields, picking up windfalls. I surprised one lady who was taking a piss behind a shed. She looked up suddenly as I came round the corner. The noise of the little two-stroke must have been masked by the rock wall. She couldn't stand up or dignify herself, or stop what she was doing, so she laughed and waved, and I pooped like a train whistle and pulled at my imaginary train driver's cord as I sped past.

The day had seemed full of promise, though not for any reason other than the colour of the morning. Perhaps also because a fisherman learns to rewrite each day with possibility. But already I could feel my confidence falter. It was my final morning, and as I leant the bike up against the picnic table and sat down to face the river I sensed the change. As though in absence I could convince myself of the promise, but in reality hope drained like a bathtub. Things were not going well between me and the Dordogne. I watched the river, waiting for a trout to rise.

After fifteen minutes, nothing. Then a dark-haired Corrèzian walked towards me along the river bank. He wore camouflage under a leather jerkin, and had a shotgun and a belt of cartridges. As he passed I said 'Ça-va?', and he said 'Ça va bien'. He stopped, looked at my shoes, at the bike, then started to speak. He stammered, and spoke with a heavy local patois – punched out words through his nose, finished them with a twang. I watched his lips jabber out long sentences and could only pick up one or two words to follow the drift of whatever he was saying; it was about the hunting season, lack of birds, the trouble with the government. He had eyebrows that closed in across his face, and only an inch or two of forehead. His ears stood out like cup handles, and one eye led off to the left, the other to the right. He made gestures, jutting out his chin, pointing to the far side of the river, scrabbling at the air with his hands. I smiled, then suddenly he took his gun off his shoulder and hammered three cartridges into it, made to fire at the trees from his hips. I was gripped with the idea that I must not turn my back on him. I wanted to get away, but felt safer listening and smiling, and he wouldn't stop. I imagined my bloodied body floating downstream, a hole in my back the size of a melon. I imagined the hatch starting just then, the current at last pocked with rising trout, as I bumped into a log midstream, face down.

Jim had warned me about this place. He'd been driving through the village one day when a horse came running up the road chased by twenty villagers – old ladies, men, children. Jim stopped his van in front of the horse, jumped out and grabbed its halter. All the villagers stopped and looked. After a while a small boy was pushed out of the crowd. He came up the road to Jim and took the horse ungraciously. Jim got back in the van, and drove through the crowd. He swears they let the horse go, and started chasing it again as soon as he had left. 'It was the best thing that happened to them all year.'

Jim's lived there for many years, is in love with the place. It's France *profonde*, he'll say. The locals have grown out of the black earth, like their maize. For me there was the river too, a big stream running through the old market town of Argentat, the town like a cubist painting, buildings carved out of the rock, a compression of stone, out of which a church tower rose. The river was a hundred yards wide, but stitched from one bank to the other with flowering water buttercup. I'd been back so many times that all my visits blurred into one, and the river always kept me at a distance. The locals gave her a personality – that of a beautiful, but capricious lover. I was here on my own this time, trying again.

The first wild trout I ever saw was in France. It's still there in mid-air, in a picture in my head. I was on holiday with my parents, their friends, and fishing with their son Warren, and his friend, Justin, I think, or Julian. J can smell fish, Warren had said, and he was a fishing god because he owned a Mitchell reel. He caught half a dozen small fish from a Brittany harbour, and cooked them on an open fire, though they tasted like a sewer and the first mouthful made me gag. The brown trout came from a rocky stream, on a float run through fast water, and I can remember the float dipping, the strike, and the fish leaping into the air.

From then on I always associated France with trout, though I've been back many times, and rarely caught one – the wrong time of year, or the wrong place. But for three summers during college I took the train south with friends from art school. We crammed ourselves into a narrow railway carriage, taking turns to stretch out on the floor, filling up on *baguettes jambon-beurre*, and coffee that made our eyes bleed, until we fell out, blinking into the southern sun of Cahors, made for a sort of artists' summer camp we'd heard of, and eroded our stomachs and morals for a fortnight of black wine and tent-hopping. Then a London cab pulled up at our den in the woods, and in it were friends of a friend, dreary pseudo-hippies for the most part, but also Juliet. I had a thing for Juliet, and I don't think it was merely lust. I was overdosing on Yeats and nurturing a sense of Celtic melancholy. She had this long hair, and a face from a painting. She was cool and she could dance. And I was young and had an erection for most of the day. So I defied my better judgement and joined the drop-outs for a drive around the hills. I remember making pasta in some derelict barn, and realising through an eight-francs-a-bottle haze that she was getting her hair stroked by one of the pseudo drop-outs. All of a sudden I didn't know what I was doing there, so I left, walked down through the woods to a gorge I'd seen earlier in the day, and cut a branch, strung it up with a hook and line, and fished with cheese in a pool between huge boulders. A railway train clattered over a stone bridge suspended high over the gorge and a few minutes later I caught the second wild trout I'd seen in France.

And when years later I came to the Dordogne for the first time, only to find her in full flood, I ended up on a nearby river running through a gorge and below a high-arched railway bridge I realised I'd been there before.

There was no fire in my head, that time. Well, a gentler one, mellowed by surety – Vicky was back at Jim's hotel. I had tagged along with Jean-Pierre, who was guiding some regular clients. We climbed from the flooded Dordogne on to the plateau of the Massif Central, and meandered south until we found a gorge so deep our ears popped twice on the way down, and Jean Pierre's worn-out Renault had an alarming case of brake fade. At the bottom we drove past the brutalist concrete architecture of a hydro-electric barrage, and parked up in the cool woods. There was clearly no hurry to the river – I'd pulled my waders on before I realised Jean Pierre and his rods from Paris were breaking out red wine, and a garlic sausage so strong that I felt sure it would ward off the vipers I'd been warned about.

'La Cère est bon, mais il y a beaucoup de vipers. Gardez,' a local on a moped had warned me the day before, as we looked over a bridge. 'They're batty about vipers,' said Jim later. 'Completely obsessed. They all go round mixing home-grown vaccines, far more dangerous than the snakes themselves. More of these guys end up in hospital each year from vaccines than snake bites.'

We lay under the trees with the Cère tumbling past, and Jean-Pierre sliced up the sausage, laid it on chunks of white bread and handed pieces around.

We rummaged through fly boxes. Jean Pierre saw

the two types of fly I'd been sold at the shop in Argentat the day before. 'C'est parfait.' One had a fiery brown collar hackle. These hackles had a sheen that you only got from Corrèzian birds, the shopkeeper had told me. Take one of these creatures to the north, and the sheen goes – and it's the sheen that attracts the trout. I listened sceptically, admired the fine-looking hackles and bought a few.

'Regardez.' Jean-Pierre picked up his rod and waded out into the first pool. 'Comme ça, est ça.' He turned the rod in the air like a conductor beating out a slow rhythm, his arm at full stretch, a fixed length of line hanging from the tip of the rod. The river fell down the gorge from one small circular pool to the next, squeezing between boulders the size of cars. Jean-Pierre got in close behind one of these pools, cast on to it with a graceful rise and fall of the rod, and then lifting gently he kept all the line off the surface as the collared dry fly floated downstream more slowly than the current. After a few casts his rod dipped and a small brown trout leapt clear of the water, throwing spray into the sunshine. 'C'est facile, non?'

I nodded, and shrugged my shoulders. 'Go, Charles, va, et attraper les truites.' He gestured me upstream, and I left him with his two pupils. The sun shone hard and split the valley in two – my bank was dark and cold, the far one shone brilliantly. Heat rippled off rocks, and ached the backs of my eyes. When I slipped into the water I felt the chill wrap itself around me. The river tumbled down past giant boulders, and where the falling water caught the sun it glistened. At the top of the run was the railway bridge.

I flicked my line on to the first pool, and lifted the rod as Jean-Pierre had shown me. I saw a copper flash in the water as a trout turned on the dry fly, and in the next pool the same happened, though this time the line straightened immediately after, and a small trout rushed around the pool.

Working up this run I felt as if I was fishing in a corridor, searching behind doors to see what was there, teasing bright creatures into the sun. I caught only small trout, though Jean-Pierre assured me there were bigger ones. I fished up under the bridge and found the boulder I'd sat on years before. I rested there for a bit watching the current in midstream, and thought about how the water just there had been flowing past from that day to this, and would be doing the same for thousands of years. In my imagination I jumped into midstream, and became a rock, and time became the river, curling round me, easing in behind, maybe a few eddies in my wake, cancelled out by those of other rocks soon enough, and then I saw the river without that rock, watched it sink and the water fold in over it as if it had never been there.

A train clattered overhead, and I carried on upriver catching trout until the sun left the water. Jean-Pierre was sitting by the river with his two clients, finishing the wine we'd opened at lunch. I asked about the chances of fishing on the Dordogne the next day. Jean-Pierre shrugged. 'The Dordogne, she is still a bad woman. She will not behave.'

I found a small stream called La Doustre, and picnicked there with Vicky and our tiny son Patrick. We drove into the valley by accident, taking a back street out of Argentat, following it across a small meadow and up a steep, wooded escarpment, until the road dropped steeply and broke out into daylight. Immediately we crossed a bridge, and I jumped out to look. In the pool downriver I could see a trout, its dark back lit up by the sun, which shone through the trees. A single-lane road followed the stream through small farms and villages, before climbing up and over the range of hills beyond, on to the vast emptiness of the Massif plateau. It was not on the way to anywhere.

The valley was narrow and bounded by steep wooded hills and outcrops of white stone mottled with moss. The river snaked through in easy curves, rattled into long quiet pools under lines of poplar and willow. Even at midday the place had the silence of dawn. I could hear Patrick shouting about tractors off in the woods somewhere, and every so often a dog barked, or a 2CV buzzed by. Over the stream dragonflies the size of toy aeroplanes swooped on the few light olives that were hatching, and along the edge thousands of water boatmen skittered across the water. Every so often one would disappear in a violent splash.

I ran a small sedge through these flotillas, and caught fat trout with coal-black spots. One old fish had a vast head and a kype on his jaw. The trout were too closely packed to get big in a little stream with long winters, but this ancient fish had seen at least eight or ten of them.

Our week unfolded changelessly, confined to side streams near Argentat, but each evening we'd walk along the quay, and sit and watch the Dordogne. She flowed hard, two or three feet up on summer level and as cold as space. We had to leave before the bad woman river would let me near her. It was just the time of year, we reasoned. Too early, perhaps. Autumn would be better than the spring.

The train from Brive to Tulle is a single-carriage diesel engine. It pulled into Brive station with a sound like a giant of the deep breaking wind. I heaved my rucksack off the station bench, along with the metal rod tube, which had been eyed suspiciously all the way from London, and climbed aboard.

I unfolded the magazine I'd picked up in Paris – *Pêche Mouche*, September issue. The front cover read: 'Dordogne, La Rivière Ésperance', and I tried to translate the first few lines. 'Unpredictable, unfishable, say the old guard. The many who come from far and wide can't hide their disappointment. Could it be that this rebellious river is so fascinating because it is so difficult to master? It is truly the river of hope.' I was riding the train south to see it again.

The carriage was full, but to my left the eight seats defined as *première classe* were empty, so I sat in one. A large brown-skinned lady in a black dress was unpeeling a boiled egg for her thin husband, who was looking at the egg carefully. She stopped as I sat. The man's eyes went from the egg to his wife, then to me. She whispered to him and he shook his head. These seats were the same as the rest, and I wondered why a republic had need of them. The train pulled out of the station and started a long climb to Tulle, diesel smoke drifting back on the wind through the hot carriage. I opened a window, and stood by it. The valley had room only for the road, river and the railway which ran up it, and on the steep sections the train slowed up enough to let me see fish rising in the pools.

Jim was on time at Tulle station. 'Ça va, mon brave,' he shouted from his Renault van. Years ago Jim bought a little hotel on the banks of a trout stream about a mile outside Argentat. There's a pontoon built over the river, where you can sit and drink a beer, and out in front the patio is overhung with wisteria. The hotel sits beside a bridge, and opposite, under the trees, local fishers and hunters tend to meet, parking their vans, chatting, occasionally strolling up to Jim's for a coffee. I guess you could say of Jim and Fi, without them minding, that they are English people gone native. Their easy company fills your head with thoughts of moving down to get a slice of the silence, and sun.

Jim fixed me up with Bernard, the president of
the local fly-fishing association. He's a good man,
said Jim – quiet and modest. Before he was due, we'd
nip along to buy a permit. It was Saturday morning, and Marie's café was busy, all the tables filled
with young men down like me to chase the grayling.
'Ça va,' said Marie, shaking Jim's hand, then mine.
'Un permit de pêche,' said Jim, and Marie dried her
hands and pulled the forms out of a drawer under
the bar.

Outside Marie's café the Pont Monceaux carries a
single-lane road high over the water. The river here
is a hundred yards wide. Behind a bridge pier a group
of trout and grayling were busy, rocking from side
to side feeding on nymphs that were rolling off the
sill of gravel under the arch. I tried to work out how
I'd cast to these fish, and after studying the depth of
the river, and the angles, realised that I couldn't. That
seemed to sum up the Dordogne. It was too big to
be a trout stream, but something made it one. Studied
in part it could be understood; as a whole it was out
of reach.

In Bernard's car we managed to talk only about
the weather. Shortly, we pulled up behind new
houses on a road that had been cut through a field,
ready for development. We strung up fly rods and
slid under a barbed-wire fence to a wood, which
ran along the edge of the river. We waded to an
island and Bernard leant his rod against a willow
bush, and tied up his tippet with two pale dry flies.

I watched, but he noticed I was ready, and gestured me to fish. I waded in and slipped into the detail of fly-fishing, watching the drift, letting the little soft hackles drag the current as they swung below me, lifting the rod with two twitches before setting the cast again. I dissected the run, trying to find those particularities that would let me understand the river. It began to rain. I looked upstream and saw that Bernard had lifted his hood and was slightly hunched against the drizzle. Puffs of smoke shone white against the trees.

After a while I waded upstream, past Bernard, who looked up and shrugged his shoulders. A trout rose in single turn, not repeated. I cast, but the drag was difficult. Nothing. Upstream ten minutes on, I saw another. I waited but the rise never came. Later Bernard tapped me on the shoulder. He had to go, he said, chores at home. I said I'd stay, but still nothing happened, and after an hour the sun burnt through the mist.

By now the day was hot, and the few rises had stopped altogether. I walked to Marie's café, ate a sandwich, drank a cold beer, and crossed the bridge to stroll back upriver to Jim's place. I could make out a few fishermen through poplars along the bank, six of them in a row. I sat on the grassy bank under the poplars now, and watched, listening to the river peeling round the anglers as they waded; the rattle of dry leaves as they slipped down the trees and on to the water, the fishermen saying 'merde'. In an hour they caught nothing, and the strong sun pressed down on the valley until everything was asleep.

I was sitting at a table under the wisteria chatting with Jim when Bernard pulled up again. I shrugged as if to ask where to? and Bernard pointed down-river. We drove in silence until the landscape changed, then made several journeys along farm tracks across fields, turning at the river and driving back through our own dust cloud, up and down the valley looking for a particular spot, until I suspected that Bernard didn't know where he was going. At last we parked in a field. Here the river lay beyond poplar trees and fish were rising up and down, as though water was dripping off the overhanging branches. I waded in, full of hope, and started to cast at the dying rings of a rise. The surface remained flat, and though I waited, nothing moved. I saw another rise a few yards upriver, and pushed slowly through the strong current to reach it. Again that rise came only once. The rises continued, but always out of reach, and it seemed once only in each spot. As I waded from one rise to the next, to wait for nothing, I had this image of Sisyphus in a river, trading his rock for a rod, for just one day, and finding that though the gods had a sense of humour, it wasn't one he liked.

Days with Bernard drifted on like this, the rise always upriver, once only, if at all.

* * *

looking at the spot where he had risen, too far away to cast, and waited for the rise I knew would not come again. And then in mid-river with the water caressing cold around my legs, I felt the rain start. I heard it drumming, and realised I was midstream waiting for a trout with my crash helmet still on.

London Trout

THE CANAL CURLED OUT OF SIGHT. IT MOVED IN pulses, the barest hint of a flow, and each pulse tilted a slab of surface reflecting slivers of sky. The sky was like dirty steel. Between the canal and the buildings was a mesh fence, rusted and broken down in places, and trees blackened with soot. A couple walked away from me. She was in a green coat, he in a suit. An older man with shining white hair walked the other way. Overhead a jogger ran across a footbridge. I heard the call of tropical birds and started walking.

Under the first bridge a man was sweeping the towpath. The writing on the wall beside him said that Jane gives it to anyone. I asked him if he ever saw fishermen on this canal, and he said that he did from time to time. Opposite us a cage leant out across the canal, suspended by poles and hawsers. Inside were bright birds, and outside men with camcorders and women with blue hair.

Round the next corner I found Kevin. He was the

far side of the canal sitting in a canvas director's chair. There was a 7Up bottle beside him and two long fishing poles leaning out across the water. Under the point of each one was a red dot. I stood opposite for a while, and watched him pull up a tiny perch, which he held in a cloth. After we had spoken for a few minutes I crossed the road bridge and climbed a fence behind him, sliding down a steep muddy bank until I was next to him on the thin strip of concrete.

'You'd be amazed what you get in 'ere,' he said. 'Round that corner I caught a bloody great perch once. I did. It was one big bastard. I got it to the edge, and leant down. I swear I couldn't get me hands round it, couldn't lift it, and it slipped back in and got off the line. It gutted me it did, cos that was the biggest fucking perch I've ever seen, ever will see.' Kevin's friend nodded.

We sat for a while longer. Kevin said, 'Caught a full set of male genitals too.'

'What? Real?'

'Real.'

'Straight up,' said his friend.

'They came floating round that corner,' Kevin nodded to the middle of the canal. 'I looked at them, and thought they looked bloody odd, so I cast out, and hooked them. Took a couple of goes, but when I reeled them in I knew what they was. I knew exactly what they was. Gave me the willies, if you don't mind the joke. So, I hung them in a bag off of that fence just there, and called the police. I said I've caught a full set of male genitals out of the canal. The copper laughed and d'you know what he said? He said "bollocks". "Bollocks"! Can you believe that? I said to him, no I really have, I've put them in a bag, and they're hooked on a fence. He believed me eventually, and they sent divers down. But they never found the body, never found who owned them. I was in the paper.'

Kevin threw out another ball of groundbait. A moment later the red dot dipped and he lifted the rod like a crane, swinging another small perch into the bank. 'Tiny. Still, we got two good roach in the net.' I asked to see them, and he lifted the net, hand over hand. Water dripped off it on to the concrete, and there in the bottom lay two roach, each about eight inches long gasping in the air, their little red eyes wide open. It was a good place to fish, said Kevin. Out of the way, a private little corner. They came down here a few times a week, and it was their spot. We talked on for a while. He asked what I was doing, and I told him I was just killing some time looking round London, at the rivers and ponds. I told him I always looked around water, wherever I was. He said he did the same.

I said goodbye, climbed back up the bank over some railings and on to a bus to Tottenham Hale. Earlier I'd been to the ponds at Hampstead Heath, and to the Serpentine looking for fish or fishermen. I'd walked the Thames too. The water had given all of these places serenity, in spite of the fumes and the sulphur-coloured sky, the old condoms and the graffiti.

From Tottenham Hale I walked to the Walthamstow reservoirs, nine windswept sheets of water within sight of Docklands Towers and in Zone 3 of the Victoria Line. The reservoirs are fed by the River Lea, and linked by a conduit called the Copper Mill Stream. The short walk from the bus stop to the reservoirs takes you over the River Lea. Two branches, one shallow and quick, the other impounded by a lock, converge downstream of the road. Along the railings above the lock were dried flowers caked in a fine film of dirt from the road. Some of the clear plastic wrapping was still tied to the railings with ribbons, and so were three grey teddy bears, and a picture of a small boy, laminated in plastic. It was curled away from me, but I could see his smile, posing I think for a school photograph, and he looked the same age as my son. The lock water was dark. There were hundreds of flowers tied to the railings, mostly dead, but some bright and fresh.

The warden at the reservoir looked at me strangely through the thick glass that protected him from anyone who might want to raid the till at gunpoint.

'You just want to look around? What for mate?'

I told him I'd heard about the grayling in the Copper Mill Stream, and that there were trout in it too – trout that had escaped from the stocked reservoirs.

'Grayling have gone, mate. Fuckin' cormorants ate

them. If you're a writer you can write about the cormorants.'

I looked behind him at a glass case on the wall. It held a large rainbow trout, and the writing said '13lb 2oz, Copper Mill Stream, 1987.' I asked about it.

'He'd been in there a few years all right. I should think there'd be others. Tell you about one we caught up in the nets. It was in one of the carp reservoirs, don't know how long, but it weighed fifteen pounds. So we put it in to East Warwick, the one down the bottom. One of those guys is going to get a fright one day. That's the club water. Walthamstow Flyfishers. But seriously, those cormorants are bastards. Over in the reservoir we have to stock trout of three pounds and up so they can't eat them. Last year I scared a bird, and as it flapped away it puked up three trout. You'll see them in the middle on the island, like a load of fuckin' undertakers in a tree. Anyway, help yourself.'

The Copper Mill Stream ran past the warden's hut and turned under a railway line. I saw one of the big chub up in the no-fishing zone, lying high in the water, along the edge. It turned with a heavy swirl when it saw me. Downstream a man in a rain-hat was peering into the water. As I approached he looked up.

'Shame, innit? You had to book to get a pitch here. All gone now, you could have it to yourself for a week. Just there I'd see big perch, but they've gone cos there's nothing to eat. Used to be 300,000 roach in here.'

I looked at him.

'Not kidding, mate, best friggin' roach river in the country. Really was. Now all those roach are ten inches of cormorant shit over on that island.'

At that he walked off, still looking into the water. I walked over to Reservoir Number One. I asked one of the anglers if he'd had any luck, but he didn't hear me properly.

'You want ticket money? Hang on a minute –' and he reached into his coat.

'No, I'm not the warden. Just wondering if you've caught anything.'

'Just startin' up. Nothing yet, but I've only just got here.'

He picked up the rod he'd just put down, and wound in the line.

'That's no good there. You've got to get it right under the trees. Right under.'

He cast again, the lead flying high. I thought it would hit the trees, and tangle.

'Still short,' he said, while the lead was in the air, and it landed with a deep thud, sending up bubbles about fifteen feet off the bank of the island.

'That's close.'

'That's not close. You've got to get it *close*. They swim right along the edge. See that branch. They lie under there, though if you get a take near it from a big boy you're shagged, he'll go right in there and snap the line.'

He cast again.

'No, short again. I need to put on a two-ounce lead in this wind.'

He wound in and opened his tackle box, and I knelt down beside him and carried on talking.

'That's some kit you've got.'

'Too right. I only took this up last year. I used to be into match fishing, but I got bored of it. It wasn't a challenge. Know what I mean? I'd catch stuff easy. Not being funny, but I just caught stuff easy. This carp game is different. You've got to work it out. They're clever. You've got to work it out. It's like chess.'

As he changed the weight I noticed a tattoo on the back of his hand: it was two rats shagging, with sweat beads bouncing off the rat on top.

'There's three grands' worth of kit here. Stupid, it really is. That rod rack costs hundreds of pounds. The bite alarm's amazing. I'll set one up in a minute.'

He picked up a jar of bait, pink balls that looked like gobstoppers.

'Pure protein this, and a smell like a tart's window box. This one's called Tangy Squid. If a carp gets a whiff of that it'll come from fifty yards off.'

He bit one in half, chewed and spat it out.

'Pure protein. Tastes disgusting. Any runs, mate?'

The fisherman from the next pitch down was walking back from the bushes behind us.

'Only in me pants.'

'Now watch. We'll sort it now.'

He cast the new bait and it thumped the water just feet from the far shore.

'Now I get the line straight, set it up in this thing, and watch the sky. Carp even breathes near my bait, and this alarm goes off. There, pull the line. Mad, isn't it? See, the way it's set up the hook isn't in the bait. The carp feels the bait, doesn't feel a hook so he sucks it in, with the hook following after, then he feels it and bolts in panic. Hooks himself.'

'Are they big, the carp here?'

'In this one they go up to thirty, over there maybe thirty-five pounds, and up the top in Lower Maynard over forty, up to fifty some say. But that's professional stuff up there. You'll fish for a year without a take, you really will. Not for me at all. Those guys bivvy up, and hide after dark, and freeze their bollocks off to catch a big one. Mad, isn't it? Mad.'

Further on I heard a bite alarm, and watched as two anglers wrestled with a carp they said was a bit of a minnow. It weighed twelve pounds, and one reluctantly held it for a picture while his mate taunted him. They told me that a thirty-five-pounder came out just a little further along a couple of hours ago. I looked along the length of the bank. It was midweek and there were twenty anglers there, some with tents, some curled up on camp beds in sleeping bags, others brewing tea. All rods pointed at the island in the middle, like siege guns.

Along the path I found a sign with an engraving showing the new reservoirs back in 1884. It was from the *Illustrated London News*, and standing at the right spot I found the angle it was drawn from. The scene along this path had hardly changed, though the line of poplar trees was now gone, along with the gentlemen in Victorian clothing, top hats at a jaunty angle. But beyond the reservoirs were fields and marshes – now there were buildings all around. Then Walthamstow had been a village, a short trip across country from the north-east edge of the city; now it was part of the city – the reservoirs a strip of water in thousands of acres of concrete. Maybe this engraving marked the turning point. The city was belching outwards even as the artist drew the scene. In 1884 there would have been trout in the Lea, but not many and not for long. The Lea, the Darent, the Wandle, Wey, Chess, Colne and Mimram – all these spring-fed trout streams were caught up in the creeping concrete and asphalt of suburbia.

I'd become fascinated by this slow death of London's trout streams. I'd been walking the canal because buried underneath it is a brook called the Tyburn. I'd come up here to Walthamstow because I'd heard about the grayling and escaped trout. Upriver was a brook called the Salmon Stream, and the Lea must once have been one of the greatest of all trout rivers. I sat by the edge of the Copper Mill Stream. I thought about the giant rainbow trout that had got fat and ended up hanging on the wall of the warden's hut. I wondered whether I'd ever find a wild brown trout. A relic of these once great rivers between upturned shopping trolleys.

*　　*　　*

I'd been asking questions. Earlier in the week a guy in the Environment Agency had told me he'd gone to Deptford Creek in east London, and there he'd found two sea trout spawning. 'It's cleaning up, you see,' he said. 'The Thames is getting better. The Ravensbourne used to be dead. There are dolphins up by Chiswick.' We talked about how Henry VIII used to keep a polar bear at the Tower and send it to catch salmon in the Thames. 'There's salmon too,' he went on. 'Some guy called Murphy rang me a while back. He'd caught a salmon on a worm in the River Wandle. In a sewage outfall, in fact.'

The River Wandle flows through south London, and was probably where I should have been looking. Catches of huge trout were once commonplace – a hundred and fifty years ago one angler caught three in an afternoon, and all weighed over six pounds. Frederic Halford, the grandfather of dry fly fishing, caught his first two trout on a dry fly there. Each weighed over three pounds. Forty years later the river was described as 'sage-green and sluggish, a sticky stream soiled by a dozen factories and smelling vilely'. It died in 1934, when its last trout was caught by a bait fisherman – a 5lb. 2oz. trout, twenty-two inches long.

Earlsfield station, one stop south-west of Clapham Junction, exits on to a busy street right underneath the railway line. The diesel clatter of traffic bounces off the brick archway. The dank air is ripe with the smell of pigeons. To the south there is a bus stop, a phone box, and a row of shops, some with boarded windows. To the north a garage, then the road curves out of sight, choked by dust and traffic. I checked my map, crossed the road and turned north, then west past a motorbike repair shop, and just beyond stopped at a small concrete bridge over the River Wandle. Below, the water was clear enough for me to see dark stones and old tyres on the stream bed, but there was that tangy, warm smell you can feel on your tongue, and the water was grey, as if someone had been washing socks some way upriver. From this bridge I could only see a few yards, so I walked back to the main road and headed south to find the Wandle Trail, a foot-path which runs up the whole river. Right opposite the station there was a tackle shop, and I went in to ask whether there were trout in the Wandle. The shopkeeper looked at me, not as if I'd asked a mad question, more as if he'd waited a long time for someone to ask it.

'They're in there,' said the shopkeeper.

The man my side of the counter agreed.

'Not many, I don't think, and no one fishes for them. You're not going to fish for them, are you?'

I admitted that I had this idea about catching a wild trout in London. He asked why, and I was embarrassed to give a reason. I don't know, I said to him, the world seems so fucked, I just think a wild trout in London would mean that it wasn't. He nodded, and I relaxed and carried on. 'Used to be loads, you know. They had a Royal Warrant on this river it was so full of trout and salmon.'

'I'm sure you're right.'

'My mate had one last year,' added the customer. 'Mostly when they do get caught, they're taken home for breakfast. Up the road the river splits in two, and there's a deep bit by the steel pilings. Try a worm along there.'

I thanked them, and as I left they both wished me luck.

I found the spot easily, a spit of land with a path worn through nettles, a shallow weir upstream which shelved down to spill foaming water into a dark pool under the trees, where the air was cold. Downstream, the two streams met, bright green weed was anchored to rubbish and its flowers swayed in the current, while a few yards away Clapham trains clattered over a bridge. There were dace on the sill of the weir, some rising to small midges buzzing over the water surface. I walked upriver all day, from Earlsfield to Carshalton, through parks, and behind factories. I saw a fox. I couldn't find any trout.

I knew of one other place I could try – in suburbia rather than the city. I'd driven through the dip of its valley many times, crossing the stream on a fast dual carriageway. The first time I'd noticed a line of poplar trees snaking away from the road, and each time after that I strained to see past the advertising hoardings, to catch a glimpse of water. I worked out from a map which river it was, and started at the bottom end. The river ran along the edge of a playing field, and under a millhouse, now a restaurant. I found a worn path and followed it to a small clearing, the remains of a fire, old bottles and mattresses. Beyond was the stream, so choked in brambles that I couldn't follow it. I had to hack in and out, peeking in to corners. Along the opposite bank large gardens ran down from a row of expensive houses, but the fences and wire made it difficult to follow there too. A large Alsatian saw me from its balcony and ran down the garden, barking. I saw a curtain flick back and forth. I fought my way back out, falling out on to the field next to a group of boys playing football. They stopped and looked at me, and walked across to the other goal to carry on their game.

I decided to get back to the car before someone called the police. It took me an hour to find the stream again. The walls and roads and cul-de-sacs of suburbia mask valley contours, and town planners bury rivers when they run across their plans. Eventually I had to ask in a garage, and the man there said I might find the stream at the garden centre down the hill.

I had to wait to see the garden centre manager. He came to the reception area of the office. 'So you want to fish for a trout in my river? How do you know there are any there?'

'I don't,' I explained. 'I'm trying to find one.'

'And what will you do, if you find one?'

'Hopefully catch it, and put it back.'

The receptionist and two office workers had gone quiet now and were listening.

'Why?'

'I just want to catch a trout. Is that OK?'

'No,' he replied, quite calmly. 'I need a better reason. Are you just checking the place out, to bring your mates along? I don't want crowds turning up looking for bloody trout, you know. I know you fishermen, rows of the buggers under umbrellas.'

'It won't be like that. Really, it won't. I doubt if there are trout there. If there are it won't be many. Look. It's just that I've been trying to find a wild trout in London. There used to be loads, you know. All the London rivers were little spring-fed trout streams, and now they're all buried, and I am just trying to find one of them that is still alive, so to speak. Just for the sake of knowing.'

'I like fish,' he said, suddenly smiling. 'Look, I've got fish all over the place.' His hand swept along the expanse of fish tanks. 'Go on, then. Help yourself. You can stay for an hour, and don't tell anyone you were here.'

Outside a bright chalk stream chattered through a culvert, and overhead trucks roared along the main road. From the culvert it split, and one branch ran to a water-mill with boarded windows. Downstream it meandered through an old park. I pulled on my waders.

'Oy.' The security guard came towards me from his hut. He'd just put down a mug of coffee. 'What the hell do you think you're doing?'

'It's OK. I've seen the manager. He said it's OK.'

'Didn't say nothing to me. What you doing? Going fishing?'

I told him about the trout.

'Yeah, yeah,' he said. 'I fish for carp. See that pond up there. Beauties in there. Trout? Tiny, aren't they. Don't know if they're worth the trouble. But start at the bottom by that tree, if you must.' He went back to his coffee.

So I started at the bottom behind the oak tree, and there upstream I found my trout. I watched it for a while, with the sound of traffic filling the breeze. It flicked side to side over stones, and once in a while it left the river bed like a kite suddenly catching the wind, until it hit the surface, and a whorl of water died away downstream. I cast once, and the trout lifted from the gravel, turned back, and hit the fly hard.

Shitloads of Refusals

JIM DROPPED ME AN E-MAIL FROM AMERICA. THE freeze-dried hippies were planning their annual pilgrimage to the Maine woods. They'd been fishing together for a long time. Nowadays they went to a river called the Penobscot, to catch landlocked Atlantic salmon. They camped by the stream, made fires, drank beer, ate moose-burgers. Jim had a spare berth in his camper van, and wondered if I'd like to join him. I asked how easy it would be to take a detour to a town called Rangeley. No problem, said Jim. We'd leave a few days early and drive up to the Rapid, a river just south of Rangeley that Jim had heard of, but never got around to fishing. He knew a guy who'd take us.

I'd been meaning to go to Rangeley for years. The Penobscot sounded great too – an all-American road trip to go fishing, drink watery beer round the campfire and shit in the woods. I'd be Kerouac with a fishing rod, and without the need to thumb a lift. I thought about it for two and a half seconds, and wrote back saying I'd be there. Jim would be dusting down the camper van in early May, and he suggested I got to his place with a day to spare, so we could get everything together.

Boston to Searsport on the Maine coast is only a short jump by plane, but Jim reckoned I should take the bus to get more of a feel for this part of America. 'You'll probably meet some whackos on the bus, and you'll get to see the landscape,' he told me.

I spent the first couple of hours leaning against the window watching the scenery unfold. I was on board with a mixed bunch – an overweight teenager wearing a T-shirt decorated with a vivid crucifixion scene and the enigmatic words READ BETWEEN THE LINES; a German couple, all in black, Flock of Seagulls haircuts; a redhead who looked mad; and a very, very fat woman. There was little to see – mostly trees and rocks, with the road winding through the clear-cut scar. I drifted in and out of sleep, woken occasionally by bursts of singing from the red-haired girl, who had her headphones on and her eyes closed. The fat woman opposite me smiled in sympathy. Later I heard the two of them talking, the large one about her ex-husband who beat her up, and her home for battered women, the redhead about her cats, and impossible parents.

When I woke again we were on the Maine coast, working our way up through fishing villages and small towns, but it was dark now, and raining. By the time I got to Searsport I was the only one left on the bus. Jim was waiting for me at the Searsport marina, hunched against the drizzle in a bright yellow oilskin.

'How was it?'

'I met some whackos, and saw the landscape,' I said.

We had a day to get our supplies together, to get Jim's camper van out from under the trees where it had stood all winter, gathering moss and leaves. I swept it out while Jim made ice.

'Everyone cooks a meal on the Penobscot. Mine's going to be a proper southern ass-smoking chilli, so we got to keep this meat good for five days.'

By afternoon we'd stored ice in the freezer, we'd been into town to tick off bread, eggs, cranberry juice, beer, a ton of sardines, and the camper was clean. But I was worried about the handgun under the bunk-bed.

'You planning on using that if I annoy you?'

'Did use it once to put a hole in a snowmobile,' he said, smiling. 'If you don't run down my apple trees you'll be OK.'

Jim is from Tennessee, speaks of some place called the Smoky Mountains as home, and has on occasion that glint in his eye.

'Anyway,' he said, 'I've got some e-mails to get away, so why don't you take off to the stream at the bottom of the hill? Just follow the path, past the pond, and you'll hear it. Cross the bridge, walk downstream, and fish back up. See you for supper?'

Jim's property extends to fifty acres of wooded valley split by a lively rain-fed brook that runs straight to the sea only half a mile downriver. I walked down as Jim suggested. The sun broke through the leaf canopy and marbled the air with patches of warmth. It smelt of moss, leaf litter, the cool dampness of the brook.

The wood gave way to a marshy floodplain, and the brook kicked off its shoes here, flowing slowly down the dark, peaty pools, leaking through the beaver dams. I sat for a while and watched the surface, soaking up the sun, waiting for signs of life. They came. A splash down from me, a splash up from me. Every minute or two a small brook trout would launch itself at the surface; the rises of hungry, competitive fish. They chased my dry fly from the bed of the river, sometimes so fast that they hooked themselves or missed it altogether.

I tried the tangled lies, looking for bigger fish. At the head of the middle pool a tree lay across a swan-neck meander in the stream. To cover the pool I had to stand up against the tree, lean over and lower my fly under the rod tip, tickling it across the surface. On the third pass a much bigger copper flash bumped the surface, taking my fly with it. The fish was only ten inches long, but it bent the rod on its tight leash and rushed for the tangled shadow under the tree. When I finally held the fish in my wet hand, I felt its cold wildness – an effortlessly beautiful brook trout.

The following morning Jim's wife Linda took a picture of Jim and me standing by the truck: two anglers destined for the hardship of the Maine woods for a fortnight, accompanied by nothing more than all the creature comforts the ingenuity of man has managed to make portable. 'We'll be fine,' said Jim, sarcastically, and Linda waved us off.

We aimed to be in Rangeley by lunchtime. Jim drove south through a handful of the Maine fishing villages and towns that I'd seen in darkness on the way up: colonial white-board housing, classical libraries and churches, tree-lined streets, and down on each waterfront a cannery for sardines, or a lobster packing warehouse. Apart from the arrival of a few high-tech businesses, there seemed to be little that would make Maine affluent, other than a landscape and lifestyle that brings what Jim calls 'leaf-peepers' snaking forth from the cities further south to spend their hard-earned cash wishing they lived in the country. Inland the tourist highways and antique shops dwindled quickly, to leave farms cut out of the scrub and forest, and the further we drove the fewer farms and the more trees we saw.

'Maine is a forest,' said Jim. 'If you don't cut your lawn for a year, there'll be a jungle under way when you turn to look at it again.'

At about 11 a.m. I saw the first signpost to Rangeley. I leant out of the window to take a picture.

Rangeley developed as a forestry town in the late eighteenth century after 'Squire' Rangeley moved up there from Derbyshire, via New York. I'd seen a family tree, and knew he was a great-great-great-great-grandfather of some sort. I have thirty-two of those of course, and realise that tracing lineage is an arbitrary exercise in self-aggrandisement. Even so, I wondered whether there'd be anything about the place, a particular appeal. I wondered whether any distant cousins still lived there. I wondered whether I'd get a free T-shirt and a discount in the shops.

We passed another sign, and then another, until we were on a quiet country lane that could only lead to Rangeley. It cut a rolling path through the trees, and to the left lay the vast Rangeley Lake, or properly Mooselookmeguntic, a place in which exploratory nineteenth-century anglers had discovered gigantic brook trout, their tails like peat-spades. The fishing was so good they built sporting cabins, and strung the fish up in rows to make postcards. They killed most of these big fish. Then finally, in an effort to enhance dwindling sport, they hammered the last nail into the coffin of Rangeley's giant brookies by stocking with landlocked salmon that knocked the food chain sideways. Today Rangeley is still famous for fishing, but it's landlocked salmon fishing – there are brookies there, and some are big, but it's not the same.

The main street – lined with telegraph poles, trees, and wooden board buildings in shades of white and duck-egg blue, their tin and shingle roofs reflecting a grey afternoon – stretched in a wide arc along the northern edge of the lake. A white church tower crowned the skyline, and nestled below it were bars, hotels, cafés and shops: Sarge's Sports Pub and Grub, the Rangeley Inn and Motor Lodge, Sugar Plums Rangeley Fudge, the Fly Box tackle store and the Parkside Café, where Jim and I ate hand-rolled burgers, drank iced tea and chatted, while I gazed idly out the window at the people of the town going about their business. I mentioned to Jim how in moments, when the scary suburban puritanism of home made me melancholic as opposed to indignant, I thought it might make sense to up sticks like the Squire, and make a new start somewhere else.

Will, the town historian met us in his clothing store. He was a short, nervous man, who moved slowly, completely focused on the reams of paper and boxes of pictures he'd assembled for us. He showed me pictures of other Rangeleys who'd visited the place, including a family from Texas all sitting round a sun lounger in the garden. I studied their picture for a long while, wondering whether we'd have anything in common. Jim looked over my shoulder and said he could see a resemblance. Before we left, Will took a picture of me, as he had of all the Rangeleys who'd visited, under the sign opposite his store, the site of 'Doc Grant's' Restaurant and half-way point between the equator and the North Pole.

We met Bob late that afternoon at Bald Mountain Camp the other side of town. We walked the bank of the Kennebago River, and retired at the end of the day for supper in the camp dining room. Bob slept in the room above me. He thumped around and snored all night. When he came downstairs at first light he said, 'That coffee and cake kept me awake till 3 a.m., revisiting the same subject – my life. Jeezus.'

'Can't do that,' said Jim from behind his curtain at the far end of the cabin.

'And d'y'know what I was thinking?' continued Bob. 'I was counting how many women I'd gotten laid with. This friend of mine said he'd gotten laid with thirty-two women, and somehow that really bothered me. I mean, I haven't had thirty-two women, and I grew up in the Sixties, for God's sake.'

'Bob, your friend counted,' I said. 'That's like counting how many fish you've caught.'

'It's worse than counting how many fish you've caught,' said Jim.

Bob poured some coffee, and settled into an armchair in the middle of the cabin. After a moment he shrugged and smiled, and started on a story about his house, about how it had been eaten by ants. He'd built it twice now. Jim joined in with the story of his new porch, and for an hour I listened to them swap house-building stories, a conversational currency you'd need to get along in rural Maine.

Bob wore shorts that hung awkwardly beneath his hefty chest and belly. He suffered from backache, and his knees and feet were swollen with the weight. But he had an easy manner, unflustered by the passage of time, a swagger which belied his boyish enthusiasm to go fishing.

'Man,' he said at last. 'We are going to *hit* those

things. There are some *big* fish out there.'

We drove for two hours south from Rangeley to meet Harry, who was joining us for the day. Harry kept the old logging dam, and watched over the river. He was a big guy, though he danced easily over the rocks. He felt obliged to watch over my efforts for a while, though I noticed Jim had sidled off down-river to fish alone. Before long, though, the inclination of all of us to make solitary progress had overcome any sense that fishing ought to be a sociable activity, and we happily cut our own courses up the river, pausing every now and then as one passed another to ask how things were going.

It took me a while to work out what to do. I was catching tiddlers when a little fish took my tip fly and dragged the dropper deep into a black pool. A large brook trout that perhaps only rarely lifted off the bottom took the dropper. I played the two of them, until an even bigger trout ambushed the smallest fish, and ate him off the end of the line. I still had the one trout, though, and played him into a back eddy off the main current, just as Jim fought through the bushes behind me.

'The big fish are deep,' I said.

'I know that,' said Jim, pointing to his rig, a vast stonefly nymph tied with two tungsten beads, a tiny green rock-worm a few inches beyond that, and a big orange bobber at the end of the fly line.

'OK,' I said, surveying his gear. 'You obviously know what you're doing.'

I held my brook trout briefly above the water, and Jim took a picture of it. Its dark back glinted in the sunlight burning through the cloud cover. I noticed the pale blue spots with red at their centre, the orange glow in the tail, the bottomless green of its fins, each edged in white, and felt the heft of its belly.

'I'm taking them on a green rock-worm,' said Jim after the fish had gone. Jim and I fished together then, dropping the heaviest nymphs into swirling dark pools, pulling up good fish, until we reached the run-down logging dam below Pond-in-the-River, where the others were waiting, casting streamers after landlocks into the white water below the dam's broken timbers and rusted iron roof.

That night at Harry's camp below the outfall we drank beer and ate sardine sandwiches and talked into the night. When Harry came down from the house the talk turned to moose. Harry stood by the door, filling the door frame, and told us about how many people get killed on Route One at night.

'You can't see 'em, that's the trouble, and they are big animals. I mean you shoot one in the woods, you'll find out how big they are. The chest's just about the height of a windshield. You quarter them, you still can't carry them. You know the best way to get a moose out? First you gotta eviscerate it . . . and I mean get on a raincoat and climb inside. Put a canoe inside that ribcage, wrap the legs round and float it out. That's the best way.'

Somehow from here the talk got round to Monty

Python and witches – perhaps we wondered whether a moose floated; like cider or very small rocks. Jim and I chuckled, but Harry went quiet and the evening lost its atmosphere. There was an uncomfortable silence, until Jim said, 'I heard a lost male partridge beating its wings this afternoon.'

Harry relaxed.

'Did you ever fire a sixteen?' he asked.

'Yup,' said Jim.

'On full auto? Man that is a weeeeeird feeling.'

'Yeah,' said Jim. 'I'd like to see one of those new anti-aircraft guns with tracking. Like a Gatling gun on R2D2.'

'I know the one,' agreed Harry with boyish enthusiasm. 'That is fast. It just zuups. That's how it goes. Zuuuup. Zuuuup. Zuuuup.'

I called home from a payphone in Greenville the next day, and spoke for too long, blowing dollar coin after dollar coin into the machine.

The camping ground owner on the Penobscot recognised Jim straight away, and began to talk to him as if he'd never left, telling him how her freezer was too full of goddam moose, and that she'd send her husband round with a few steaks for us boys later on that day. Jim said he was going to cook a proper southern ass-smoking chilli, and she replied drily that we needed to watch out for the bear that had been poking around the latrine lately.

'Oh, I think my chilli will get rid of him,' said Jim.

Barney was tucked under the bonnet of his flat-bed at the entrance to our campsite.

'Hey, Jim,' he said turning his head, but too wrapped in cable and grease to stand up. 'Distributor's playin' up.' Barney runs a Hazard County flat-bed, which, according to Jim, breaks down every year.

Down the slope from here half a dozen tents surrounded a clearing in the trees, overlooking the river. At its centre was a table laden with mustard, ketchup, crisps and beer. A bin-bag, already half full with crushed beer cans, hung from a nail in a tall pine that leant out over the water. A fire smouldered below it, and either side of the lazy column of smoke were two figures, their backs to us. One stood, rocking from foot to foot, a can of Bud in one hand, a cigar in the other. The other, slumped in a camping chair, burped loudly.

Jim called over, 'Shawn, you reprobate, you have begun drinking without us.'

Shawn turned, laughing wildly, his eyes set against the drift of cigar smoke.

'Hey guys, how's it going? Come have a beer.' He shook my hand warmly, with one of those bonecrusher grips that told of his days as a football pro, as much as the downhill migration of his muscle bulk told of his days since retirement. 'Pleasedtameet ya, Charles. Here, meet Chuck.'

Chuck could have been Shawn's son – he was

twenty years younger, and wore his baseball cap backwards. He lurched upwards, slurred out a hello, and fell back into his seat again. Chuck was tanked, and it wasn't even mid-afternoon. That night he vanished into the woods to look for bears, then later tried to dock in the wrong tent, before finally collapsing in a heap with his Goldfish potato snacks. He didn't get up until noon the next day. It may have been a rite of passage, for after that he no longer felt the need to outdrink a generation of Woodstock veterans who had blown their livers long before he was born.

'The other guys are at Ass Rock,' said Shawn.

'Brought my brother here last year,' said Jim as we searched the undergrowth for the right path. 'And I told him, it's Ass Rock, cos you sit your ass on it, and don't move. I had to go keep fetching him, and putting him back there. Soon enough though, he found out that the fish move past you, not the other way round.'

Marcel, Will and Norm were all there, taking it in turns to fish heavy nymphs through the run off the rock, but they all stood aside to let me have a go.

'Welcome to Ass Rock, Charles,' said Will. 'Throw the heaviest nymph you've got no further out than under the rod tip.'

The river heaved over a shelf of rock above us and slid sideways over cobbles straight towards our bank, where it met an unyielding rock face, folded up on itself, and slid away downstream. We stood at the fold, and in the deep channel that had been cut by the roiling water the fly bounced around like a balloon in an updraught. I passed it through the run two or three times before the line stopped and I came into startling contact with my first landlocked salmon. The rod tip jangled about as though a rubber ball were tethered to the other end, and suddenly a careening, effervescent creature burst into the daylight and danced in front of us. It skipped on its tail, vanished, jumped again in another place, and kept at it until I pulled hard on the rod, and slid the fish towards me over the water.

'Hey Jim, this English pal of yours is not such a dumbwit after all,' said Marcel.

It wasn't a great year for the landlocks: for a reason no one could identify, the smelt on which they usually feed were not running the river, and the landlocks were smaller and thinner than usual – reduced to feeding on caddis, and mayflies, like resident trout. We tried fishing with streamers a few times, the classic Carrie Stevens patterns tied to imitate smelt, but caught very little that way. Instead it was upstream work with dead-drift nymphs, or dry fly in the evening through hatches of caddis, when pools like Stonefly Heaven would burst into life as the last light faded upstream.

Unlike Jim and Will, I had no experience to jade

my feelings about what was in front of me right now. Jim missed the seventeen-inchers of previous years, but soon adapted his Rapid River technique, sufficient to winkle the biggest landlocks from lies so fast you'd suspect little other than a rock could hold in them. Annoyingly I fished all of this water ahead of him, catching nothing. I turned at regular intervals to see Jim's rod bent hard over, and only occasionally was it because he was stuck on the bottom. His finest fish broke off midstream, and Jim blamed it on the irrepressible Chuck.

'He jumped just as Chuck screeched "way ta go" from the other bank, and that seemed to annoy him somewhat. He took off with a vengeance and broke my line. That was a two-foot salmon. A real nice one. Bloody kids.'

One hot afternoon I found myself alone on a piece of bank some distance from the road. The sheer blue sky, like a hollow dome over the river, was split down its centre by the vapour trail of an intercontinental jet. It was hot enough to crack drying timbers in the wood behind me. Once in a while the thumping, hollow rat-a-tat-tat of a woodpecker overplayed the constant rasping of the blue jays, whose metallic trills sounded like the sharpening of knives. The river rushed beside me. Away in the distance I could hear Shawn roaring with laughter.

The river came alive. A blizzard of caddis burst into the dry air and I spent the afternoon working a run only thirty yards long, never once casting blind. I caught only two fish, but one was as long as my arm and had me dancing over rocks to keep up. With more bulk to him he'd have got off, but after an exhausting burst of speed I brought this glorious salmon to hand. It was big enough to really look like a salmon. One whose ocean had been reduced by geology and mankind to large rivers and lakes, yet still a salmon. With the added complexity that they feed in fresh water, they are just as maddening to fish for. When I got back to the campsite that evening and asked Chuck how he'd got along, he summarised the experience: 'We got shitloads of refusals.'

We ate venison steaks, and duck breasts basted in garlic, the outsides barely seared in the heat of the campfire, the insides running red. Marcel was *chef de la maison*, in the sense that he barked out urgent instructions no matter what was going on, or who was cooking.

'You're doin' all right, Charles,' he said to me. 'When Jim told me he was bringing some English guy over called Squiggly-Fuckwit, I thought oh Kerist, he's gonna be calling the Queen to come rescue him in her helicopter, he's gonna cry and wanna go home. You might make it, though.'

Barney was standing with his back to the fire, his arse inches away from the heat of the flames, wreathed in smoke, laughing silently into the night: a joint was doing the rounds. Norm wrestled with the music box.

'How the fuck do you work this thing?'

'Short side to the right,' said Barney, his eyes half closed, lifting a styrofoam coolie to his mouth. A bouncing chord tremolo cut through the silence of the woods. Barney acquired an air guitar, and Marcel closed his eyes and tapped his feet. Shawn began gyrating his hips, while Norm bounced up and down and shouted into the dark, 'Fuckin' Waylon Jennings, man!'

We talked about knives, ageing, back-yard snow-blowers, whether the butterflies which seemed attracted to the spots in the trees where we'd peed were attracted by the sugar, or salt, about fly-tying, and how you shouldn't insult salmon by presenting uncomplicated flies to them, about Outlaw music, and Nashville hegemony, about Annie Proulx's book on making cider, rambling on until a gentle but persistent rainshower turned the table-top to a mess of napkins and watery pools of ketchup. The fire burnt out, and we each drifted off to bed.

Ten days in the woods, and a diet of raw meat had me missing Vicky in all the usual ways. Talk on the drive home was all about our top ten hypothetical shags – actresses and singers. There was surprising agreement on the unfortunate objects of this camp-site lust. Sandra Bullock for one.

'She grew up on her father's log yard, kicked the shit out of all her brothers,' said Jim. 'Just makes your eyes water thinking of her loading logs in a denim shirt, her trousers slowly unravelling up to the tops of her thighs.'

'How about Madeleine Stowe?' I asked.

'Good choice,' said Jim.

'She's really hot in *Twelve Monkeys*. Helena Bonham-Carter too.'

'Interesting choice,' said Jim. 'Personally I'm crazy about an overbite and cup-cake tits. That's why Gwyneth Paltrow is top of my list.'

'I need to get home,' I said.

Jim agreed. We were getting too pathetic for our own good.

Jim waved me off at Searsport marina, gave me a copy of the *Camden Times* property pages, and said he hoped I'd had a good time. Ironically, I had Sandra Bullock's thighs to marvel at all the way back to Boston – the bus TV had *Miss Congeniality* as main feature – a banal movie, enlivened only by my own superimpositions of logging yards and unravelling denim.

We swung out on to the north–south coast road, past Mr Tire and Co. Bullets and Bait, and a garage sign 'We're praying for Joddy Rae – we love you.' I looked at the signs again as we passed through Camden, then Belfast: 'Don't be fooled – kinder is not wiser' or 'John Fence – all types of fencing.' It's strange how a sign can summarise a place. In the back of my mind I'd wondered on this trip what it would be like to live here. The signs, like the place, were fresh, and attractive. Back home signs fade into the landscape, as they would here once you were used to them. And beyond that point, I thought, when all that freshness was just normal, I'd need to be sure it was a better normal than the one I had already.

New Red Land Rover

A SONG BY NATALIE MERCHANT GOES LIKE THIS:
'Climbing under a barbed wire fence by the rail-
road ties, climbing over an old stone wall I am
bound for the riverside. Well I go to the river to
soothe my mind, ponder over the crazy days of my
life, just sit and watch the river flow.'

The last thing my mother said to me was, 'I'm
glad you got your Land Rover sorted.' My dad and
I had just been out to collect it from the guy who
fitted it up – a salvaged engine in a galvanised chas-
sis with a mix-up of body panels, all red on the outside, different colours on the inside and under the
bonnet. I'd driven up to collect the Land Rover and
see my parents. My mother was OK the day I arrived,
though she had lost weight, and she climbed the
stairs slowly early in the evening. The next morning
she felt ill, and she was sick all day. Late afternoon,
when she was asleep, we went out to fetch the Land
Rover, and when I got back that is what my mother

said. She didn't want me to stay, and she was too tired to talk, so I went downstairs to work for a while, and an hour or so later I heard her dying. We weren't expecting it right then, but it's like a train you've never seen before and may not recognise, and though you know it will come, you don't know when. You find yourself sitting in the station, not wanting to look up the line.

She looked hot, so I wet a flannel and put it on her forehead. She opened her eyes briefly. I sat next to her, and read her a prayer from a book by her bed, and as I reached the end of it she stopped breathing. I can hear her last breath. She wasn't old.

The prayer said 'We seem to give them back to Thee, O God, Who gavest them to us. As Thou didst not lose them in giving, so we do not lose them by their return.' It was the first I found, and it seemed right. I left the room then, so my dad could be on his own, and went downstairs to make supper. I opened a tin of tomato soup, and leant my head against the cold brick wall next to the cooker as I stirred it. I didn't want the soup, and I wondered if I'd get to sleep that night. I wasn't looking forward to the night. I tried to believe that this empty, heavy space in my chest was all I needed to be sad for – the absence, that either I believed or I didn't, that the body taken downstairs and out the front door in a black zip-up bag had simply let her down – that now she was somewhere else. That I'd miss her, that's all.

New Red Land Rover

The day after, I had to drive to London to tell my grandmother that her daughter had died. As I turned on to the A10 this reassurance left me, and I pulled over and shouted and hit the steering wheel until my throat cracked and my hands hurt.

In October on a fishing trip this all came back. Not for any reason that I can think of – it just did because on the road the tide is out for long enough. Autumn brings round these thoughts. It is a time when life draws into itself, and continues beyond sight. You have to dig down into the earth or scratch at bark to see it. This time it hit me harder than ever before – in such a way that afterwards I wondered where I'd hidden it all this time. I was in the same red Land Rover, doing too much thinking, and I thought about my mother, and how I wanted to talk to her. It was as though I drove into a fog bank. I could barely see, and I slowed into the inside lane. After a while a car overtook, and the passengers in it turned to look at me. It jolted me and I picked myself up, and drove on.

As the song says, the river flows.

The Edge of the World

I'VE FOLLOWED THIS BLUE LINE BEFORE, IMAGINING what was there. And on the bank at Fizzy Bridge I've often looked upriver, at the zigzag of drain fading towards an indistinct vanishing point, disguised by the shimmer of heat in summer, or by mist in winter. October last year two kids out on push-bikes with their fishing rods told me about a lake in the trees up there to the south of the drain: 'Massive pike in there,' one said. I could see a copse way off in the distance.

'Whose fishing?'

The oldest grinned and said, 'Never asked.'

It's just down the road. I can see the flood bank across the fields from the window I'm sitting at. I could be looking out to sea, and would have been a few hundred years ago, before the land was drained. But it's still as untouchable; though you can cross the place on the buckled shipping lane of a fenland road, the ghost of the sea is there. Some mornings it feels like you could drown out there.

There are fish here at Fizzy Bridge. I saw one when I found the place last autumn. The sun was low in the sky. I caught a glint of striped emerald close to the bank, suddenly eclipsed by my shadow, the heave at the surface of displaced volume, a billowing cloud of silt.

Three hundred yards up the flood bank a pipe crosses the drain. The flow falls fractionally, and over the years has coaxed a deeper slot from the uniformity of an engineer's drawing. There's a big pike in there too. It's as far as I've walked.

The blue line scythes lazily on the map, six miles from one bridge to the next. Nothing between them, though one never knows. I spread the map out on the table and this new place stood out as surprisingly as if someone had changed the topography and sketched it in. The map showed a sharp kink in the drain, north, then west again. Off each kink a cut-off channel. A few yards downstream a narrow bridge. On the Fens you look for features like these. Shoals of bait-fish congregate near bridges and any other subtle change to the monotony of the man-made channels. The pike follow.

The map showed a track too, saving me a three-mile hike up the flood bank.

I drove in past an empty camp ground washed over by the grey morning, a Mr Whippy ice-cream sign splashed with mud, leaves licked into corners by equinoctial winds. Further on I passed a corru-gated tin house, fossilised in layers of gloss green paint. An Alsatian spun ferociously on his chain, front legs rearing off the ground as he barked at the limit of his restraint, the ground worried away to bare dirt in a perfect circle around him. Three fat white ducks sat under an apple tree in the yard, then stood and waddled away as my front wheel dropped into a rut in the road and splashed water over the fence. The rusted hulk of a Bedford truck was buried up to its hubcaps. A sycamore tree threaded through the cab.

At the end of the track I reached the gaunt remains of a priory, its main arch and a few walls propped up by scaffolding poles. Beyond stood a dark stone farmhouse, spotted here and there with inserts of carved white blocks ransacked from the crumbling priory. I saw a collie asleep in the concrete yard, and walked up quietly. Eyes on the collie, I missed a border terrier, which bit my ankle. The collie woke, barked, and waggled its tail. I patted the collie, and kicked the terrier.

'You got that right,' said a voice from the shed in front of me. 'He's soft, that one. But watch the other.'

'Hello,' I said, peering into the dark. 'Yes. He got my ankle.'

'Did he now? He's good at that. Postman stops at the end of the track now. Says he won't come no further. Had to put a box up.'

'You the farmer then?'

'Not me, no. Odd jobs, that's all. I'm fixin' this heater right now. Bloody thing. But it's a runner, I'm

sure. No point throwing that out for want of a little attention.'

'Suppose not,' I said, looking at it, tapping the
edge with my toe. 'Anyway, I'm here to ask about
the fishing. Wondering if I can go down to the drain
across this land here.'

'Well you'll have to ask Mr Jacks. That'll be his
say-so.'

'Is he about?'

'I'll see if I can find him.'

He knocked on the back door of the farmhouse,
which was quickly opened by a breathless lady in
leopard-skin pants. Her blue top was pulled tight
across her chest, and a necktie of sweat separated
her breasts.

'The man here wants to know if he can go fishing.'

She turned to look at me. I smiled, and looked at
the ground.

'Wait here.'

She turned and went back inside. A moment later
Mr Jacks appeared. He had a smile on his face.

'Course you can,' he said. 'You can go up to the
end of that hedge over there. What you fishing for,
then?'

'Pike.'

'Oh yes. Pike. Now then, they're ugly brutes are
they not? There's one just above the bridge.'

'If I catch one would you like it to eat?'

'Well, they say they're good, I know, but I tried
one once and didn't get along with it too well. I

nearly killed myself on those bones. Didn't think much of it at all. It was muddy too. Not for me, no. Off you go then.'

He closed the door on me. The odd-job man shrugged. I followed the path to the river.

Discovering new water is as intriguing three miles from home as it is three thousand. The river here is buried deep inside a cut in the land, and I heard it before I saw it. You rarely hear Fen water, so I was straining my neck as I climbed the flood bank, keen to get a look. The drain ran clear, and flowed either side of the pier of an ancient footbridge, pulling weed tight in the current, curling on into a flat pool, fifty yards long, through another brick pinch, and then down a fast chute. Two pools, tongues of current, back-eddies, slack run-outs. I'd find fish here for sure.

I walked the edge, saw a jack pike and a large trout. The trout amazed me. I'd heard, but hadn't known whether to believe, that sea trout ran this drain. To do that trout would have to drop down from the hills miles away, where the drain is a river. This proved that they did or could. From my back door I can see a sugar beet refinery, a railway line, and at night the flicker of lights on an industrial estate; they'd have to swim past all of that too. Where the stream runs into the sea, it passes a housing estate. I went there once, looking for the sea trout, but the place was covered in dog turds and graffiti, and from a warehouse I'd heard a crowd of people shouting 'one two, one two, huh, one two, one two, huh.' I'd never plucked up the nerve to fish there at night.

Upriver I walked the two bends I'd seen on the map. Between the bends alongside a reed-bed the water dropped away to dark shadow. The pike appeared suddenly on the second cast, following my fly right across the channel, before halting at the near edge, its fins alert. I pulled again and the pike followed once more and stopped. Then one more time, and I saw the red of the gills as the pike opened its jaws. It hammered forward, took in the fly, and continued upriver until the line tightened under the rod tip, the pike exploding with confused fury. I felt my legs go light, my ears pound.

I scrambled down the bank to bring it to hand. A perfect pike, marbled in light green, fat and deep, with a tight head. It must have grown quickly on ducks and trout. I climbed back up the bank, and sat down to watch the fish recover. The drone of a gravel works drifted across the flat land on the breeze, like the rush of water on a beach. A mile away I could see a circular tower, and piles of aggregate. When I released the pike I caught its muddy scent on the grass bank, and in the copse where I'd hung my coat.

Beyond the gravel works a line of pylons runs down the valley, following the drain. They tower over the land like the menhirs of Easter Island. Sometimes I see patterns of line, crossing, and recrossing, like a vast metallic web. At Fizzy Bridge electricity crackles in the air like an untuned radio.

The Fens are charged with this friction.

I saw another pike here later that day and called Jonathan to tell him about the luck I was having. He found an excuse to head north, and that weekend we walked the flood bank while the tips of our heavy fly rods bent sideways in the wind. 'You know it's going to be easy when this happens,' shouted Jonathan. The water was up, but clear; high enough to flood the grassy margins at the base of the incised bank. Jonathan went ahead, and within minutes was into a pike of about six pounds. It twisted and shook at the surface, and threw water into the wind, which lashed the spray back down again, like someone had thrown gravel. 'Bugger,' said Jonathan – the pike was gone. But six yards on he took another, this a little bigger than the first.

A tuned Ford Escort pulled up at the bridge – I noticed the oversize exhaust, the squat stance of the car. Three lads sat inside until the windows steamed up. Then they climbed out and leant on the parapet, watching us. Jonathan gestured me to go ahead after his third fish, and I covered the last few yards to the bridge, until the fly was landing right underneath them. I prayed for a fish. And as they watched in intimidating silence a black shadow separated itself from the river bed and moved over the white of the fly. The front of the shadow shook, and I lifted up as hard as I could. 'It's a big one,' I called back to Jonathan. The pike bent my fly rod into a hoop. 'That's fourteen or fifteen,' reckoned Jonathan, dragging on a ciggy at my shoulder. The racers joined us on the flood bank.

'Fuckin hell, that's a big fish,' said the driver. They watched me tow this fenland crocodile uselessly up and down. It hung limp like a deadweight, then erupted into life, then hung limp again, until it surged through a weed-bed and left the fly behind. The crocodile turned slowly on its axis, like a compass needle, and watched us from the river bed. The racers drifted away. 'Let's go,' one of them said. 'It won't come again.'

I watched the fish for a while.

'Come on,' said Jonathan. 'Let's go get a pint.'

We drove to Welney, cutting out across the fenland sea, Jonathan's car roiling like a fishing smack over the tarmac. The coastline of low hills faded behind, until it seemed obvious that the world was flat. The flood banks of the Bedford Levels reared up like an archipelago; along the shore, the burntout wreckage of stolen cars.

'A kind of local hobby,' I said.

We crossed the Bedford Level, an eerie strip of wetland between the channels. Welney is anchored here.

The pub had a tiny front room, its white walls lacquered yellow by cigarettes. A wooden bar jutted out into one corner. A small fire glowed weakly in the grate, filling the room with smoke and the smell of peat. Jonathan ordered two pints of mild. We sat down next to an upright piano, beside two old men in suits.

'Been fishing, lads?' asked the man in black with a cap.

We told them we'd been after pike, but that most had got off the line.

'Love pike, I do,' said the other.

'Fishing for them, or eating them?' I asked.

'Well both, and one's got to come before the other.'

'Don't know,' said his friend. 'My opinion is that they're slimy.'

'Well my wife makes a fish pie with pike. It's a beaut.'

'How does she cook it, then?' I asked.

'Big dish. You got to lay the pike, then potato, then pike, then potato, and cover it all with a cheese sauce. Bloody fantastic. That'll get me home from the pub.'

'But they're slimy buggers for sure,' said the man in black, turning to us. 'You eat one without draining off the slime, they'll taste of mud, if that's not an insult to mud.'

'You use salt, don't you?'

'And tons of it. Lay that pike in a salt bath overnight, and it'll draw all the snot off. But don't pour that down your sink, cos no plumber on earth will fix it if you do. Then soak that pike in fresh water, and change it as often as you can be bothered. You'll clean it up then.'

We drained our pints and bought two more, with bags of peanuts. 'Forget lunch,' said Jonathan. 'Let's go and catch one of those fish.'

Outside the wind cut across the wet fields, and I shivered. A bank of cloud was building out to the east, and the light had faded to a steely grey, reminiscent of winter days that end with snow.

'We'll give it half an hour. After that I reckon my nads will have shrunk to nothing.'

We set out along the bank, heads down against the wind. The men in the pub had told us about a big fish under the willow, opposite the longboat. I tried here while Jonathan walked further. A small pike hit my fly, and a while later another turned near it, but somehow we could tell the day was over. The cold was thinning my blood. This narrow channel had a chop to it that was frothing the water in the pony drink. It was an effort to cast.

'Let's go,' Jonathan said. He'd lit up, and didn't care if there was a big one uncaught. We walked up to the top of the embankment. The wind ripped over the Fens, reared up the steep bank, and howled into the abyss. The Hundred Foot Drain and the River Delph were over their banks, and as far as we could see the fields were under water, a grey patchwork, stitched by hedgerows.

'The edge of the world,' I said.

'It's bloody fantastic,' said Jonathan. 'Another country.'

I told Nick about the big fish that came off, and we met at Fizzy Bridge, surprised to find Portakabins and diggers all over the place. The man in the booth on the bridge said, 'Don't park there, mate, you'll get flattened. Try up the road.' When we walked back he came and leant over the edge with us. 'Anything in there, then?' A few, we told him, though I was worried all this work might have chased the fish upriver. The water was clear, and we quartered down to the reed-bed above the bridge. Nick was back at the car when I hooked it. I saw the pike come right across the channel and stop behind the fly. This vast fish opened its jaws and docked the fly like a mother ship. The man on the bridge called to Nick, 'Your mate's into one.' The driver behind me turned off his engine.

'That's a big one,' said Nick when he came back. Then he put on his shades and said, 'That's a really big one.'

'How big?' I asked.

'The one you've got on has got to be fifteen, but the one following it looking hungry is twenty, easy.'

We got mine on the bank, and posed it for a picture. The digger driver said 'Bloody hell', and Nick agreed it was bigger than we thought. 'That's closer to twenty than fifteen. Eighteen, maybe.'

And we both turned to look back into the water. 'If this one's that size . . .'

'I know,' said Nick. 'It's five inches longer. That's a bloody great fish in there.'

Big White Knickies

OUR WEEK WAS OVER. WE'D BEEN LOOKING FOR THE unicorn, but we hadn't found it.

It was still dark when our ferry docked on the mainland – we drove through the cold without talking. As the unwashed world took shape beyond the headlights we spoke occasionally about where else we could have been, had we chosen better. Maybe we could end the week with a fish after all. I pulled over by a phone box as we drove alongside Loch Lomond. The road was wet with leaf fall and smelt of autumn, but the phone box smelt of piss and tobacco. The season had one more day left to run, so I called a keeper on the River Lyon, who told me a sixteen-pound hen salmon had been caught the day before, that we could book the beat for tomorrow if we wanted it. But Richard, who had seemed briefly encouraged by the idea, looked at the trees and the water, or beyond them. After a moment's pause he said, 'That means *we* won't catch it.' He stayed in the car. I walked back to the phone box, and told the keeper to forget it.

Further south we pulled into a service station, ordered two coffees, and sat in plastic chairs next to a fountain. Fat cherubian mermaids spat water into a shallow pool filled with coins and cigarette butts. Insipid music leaked out of speakers in the ceiling. Richard sipped his coffee, slouching back, his eyes still unfocused, and said finally, 'They have to be the most elusive bloody fish in the whole world.'

'They are,' I agreed, knowing that he meant elusive for the best and worst of reasons. Spectral was good, absent was not. The expectation of sea trout is a frag-ile hope nowadays. Richard was staring at his coffee.

'What's wrong?'

'This is really bloody awful,' he said, and pushed it away.

I felt bad. When I'd mentioned this place I really thought it would work. I can take or leave the nomadic beasts a lot more easily than Richard, who is addicted, and this week had stretched him out on the rocks. We sat watching the fountain for a while before I stood to go. As I did, Richard looked at me.

'It's funny, you know, but in some ways I'm going to miss Duncan. Nothing else. I'll never go back. The place is a dump. But Duncan has got to be one of the best ghillies I've ever met.'

Seven days earlier we'd driven off the ferry on to a greasy black road that had faded into indistinct distance, and in the few seconds it took to assimilate the landscape, we both knew without saying that we'd imagined somewhere else. It shouldn't have made any difference, but somehow the place and the weather picked at the seams of what we'd been hoping for. Low cloud hung like a headache, and something more than mist and less than rain fell slowly, blurring the sky with the land. What we were looking for didn't exist. The whole thing seemed to me in that moment the construct of a past that had vanished, and our memories of it that had grown romantic, and absurd. We watched a puddle out of a side window, the surface taut, vibrating, suddenly furrowed by wind racing across it. The squall licked across the road and rocked the car, throwing water up against the glass. We sat listening to the engine, the wipers, the rain.

'Fucking hell, this is a dump,' said Richard, annoyed with himself for believing, even for one second.

Up ahead a line of street lights threw dirty orange haloes into the sky. The phosphorescence caught lone blockhouses, each enclosed by a scrubby paddock lined with dry-stone walls. Sagging wires held up by rows of wooden pylons cross-hatched the land like a spider's web. I dropped the clutch. We drove through a landscape dotted with bungalows, abandoned cars, roofless stone crofts. Strips of leaden water broke the expanses of heather and bog.

At the end of the island we dropped down a shallow hill towards a harbour. We passed a boat in a field, a new department store and flats, empty and For Rent. It was low tide and three fishing boats lay on the mud under a heavy sky, blistered by rain. The trees on the hill had grown crooked, leaning back from the shore, beaten into shape by non-stop westerly gales. On an outcrop of land overlooking the bay stood our hotel.

'Shit.' Richard stopped and looked back across the bay. 'I can imagine the Vikings landing here, taking a look around and buggering off again. It is an unremitting hole.'

A smell of dead fish and diesel oil blew off the greasy rocks at the waterfront. I tried to ignore it.

'Dunno,' I said. 'It's raining. Wait till tomorrow.'

The hotel reception desk was deserted, so we hung around the hall for a minute or two. I looked at the stuffed sea trout on the walls. Huge fish, caught recently, not a hundred years ago. I perked up and nudged Richard. 'I'll fish off the devil's ringpiece if it means catching fish that size.'

Just then a lady opened a door into the reception office. 'Hello. How can I help you, gentlemen?' She had her hair up in a bun, and blue kohl drawn clumsily across her eyelids. The voice was high and indifferent, the words entirely separated from their meaning. We said we were expected, explained who we were. We followed her to the hotel annexe, a prefabricated metal hut, down a corridor lined with framed sea trout flies and frilly pink curtains. It smelt of damp, and pine air-freshener.

'There you are, gentlemen.' She sighed slowly, as though some difficult task was over. After a pause we said the rooms were nice. She nodded again, and walked away down the corridor. Richard looked at me and raised an eyebrow. When she was gone he threw back the curtain and said, 'Look at the view, Chuck. You can see some water if you crick your neck.'

'Well we're here,' I said. 'We've got to give it a chance. Those fish in the hall . . . I mean if there are sea trout like that . . . and the place could be crawling with them. One fish like that, I'd sleep in a shithouse at the end of the garden.'

And the morning was brighter. Sun shone through gaps in the clouds and picked out colours we hadn't seen on the fishing boats and the hills. We looked through the window at the changing light while we drank our coffee, and we felt better. A full day lay ahead, with all the immeasurable possibility of fishing. As we chatted, a blue Ford Escort patched with filler, and bulging at its rusted seams, pulled up in the car park. A man stepped out holding a set of yellow oilskins and a plastic bag. He stood next to the car, rolling a cigarette.

'Reckon that's our ghillie,' I said. We finished our coffee.

A cap embroidered with a red and gold moose drew a line above his pale eyebrows, weathered skin and thin lips. He wore black shoes, suit trousers, a frayed roll-neck sweater.

'Duncan?'

'Aye. And you're Charles, and Richard isn't it?' he asked, shaking our hands. 'Now we're going to have a good week, are we not?' He looked at the two of us. 'Come on, let's be going. These fish dennae wait, you know. We'll stop at the store for supplies.' And he walked over to the back of our car, where he'd placed an outboard motor, and leant against it while we got our stuff together.

The store was set back from the road, with a pot-holed car park out front. Richard and I bought bread and cheese, arguing as usual about white versus brown, Cheddar versus Primula – 'It's Primula, not Prime-uler. God you make it sound like window putty.' 'Well it bloody tastes like window putty' – but we were back in the car before Duncan came out. He was carrying two full bags of shopping.

'Duncan's bought some stuff,' said Richard. But he walked the other way, followed by a prim lady in brown shoes with glasses, curly hair and a heavy coat. He put the shopping into her car boot. Richard pulled open a packet of crisps. 'Nice chap. Just helping that lady with her shopping. Must have his lunch in his pocket.'

Duncan walked back to our car, smiling, and leant in Richard's window. I didn't catch what he said, but Richard did.

'Oh God!' said Richard, spraying his crisps over the back of the seat. 'Duncan, that is disgusting.'

'Try telling her that. Now off we go.' And with

that he climbed in, and pointed out of the car park. At the next crossroads he asked us to turn left. 'Dat's vere she divvs.' His mouth full of chocolate, he pointed to a large house on the corner. It stood below the road, stained by weather and moss and leaky gutters. In the garden a washing carousel decked with expansive white underwear spun in the wind. He groaned slightly as we passed it. A little way down the road, still looking over his shoulder, Duncan fumbled for the handle on his door, dropped the window half an inch, and held the chocolate wrapper in the wind until it blew out and landed on the tarmac behind us. Richard turned to watch it fall.

'Pull over up ahead.' We had come along a single-lane road between two small lochs. Duncan stepped out and opened a gate into a field to beckon me forward. While he was out of the car Richard leant over and whispered, 'This man is mad.'

I leant out the window.

'Looks rough.'

'It'll be fine.'

'You aren't the one who signed the collision damage waiver thingy.'

'You'll nae collide with anything in here.'

I drove on, over the brow of a hill, and the engine sump caught a rock.

'That'll do.'

'We've knackered the sump to save a hundred-yard stroll.'

'You carry this bloody engine a hundred yards.'

Duncan heaved the outboard out of the back, and set off down the hill to his boat. I looked at Richard and shrugged.

The loch water was brown like stewed tea. Light wind blew in across the western shore, and the air smelt of rotting bladderwrack. All around, bungalows and crofts interrupted the line of low hills. 'You'll use a Goat's Toe,' said Duncan. 'Think I have one here.' He opened a rusted tobacco tin, stirring the flies inside with a calloused finger. They were all Goat's Toes. 'We'll stop at the post office later, where you can buy your own.'

Richard wanted to use a Bibio. Duncan shrugged and said, 'Suit yourself. But a Goat's Toe is the fly.'

I tied the fly on and started to cast. As we drifted, the wind chopped waves into the back of the boat. I settled into the ritual of loch fishing, the familiar beat taking over, in time with the waves, the whole process buoyed up on a sense of hope that comes naturally as soon as the line swishes back and forth. Across the easy sound of the water and my fly line, Duncan whistled tunelessly. He whistled at a flock of black sheep on the hill, an idle distraction at first, which he repeated until it became disturbing. The sheep paid no attention to him. I caught Richard's eye, made a puzzled face. Suddenly Duncan sneezed, and the sheep bolted over the hill.

'That's your sheep gone, Duncan.' He didn't react.
'Will you look at that, 'tis a splay-legged goshawk.'
'A what?'

'A splay-legged goshawk.' Duncan nodded towards a seagull. 'Why does it have splay legs?'

Richard shrugged. 'I don't know. Why does it have splay legs?'

'Because it lays very large eggs.' Duncan laughed quietly.

'Oh help,' Richard groaned.

We fished through the morning. Duncan chuckled to himself and his jokes got worse. The Goat's Toe was a tiny psychedelic squid of a fly. It bobbed through the waves, leaving a wake in the oily brown water. I lost track of time, but around midday a tail fin cut through the froth and slid under again as my line straightened. We had drifted close in against the rocks. I instinctively lifted the rod, thinking as I did that I'd missed the fish. But the rod bent against a heavy weight, which held for a moment. The weight shook from side to side. Then the line went limp. Richard and Duncan had stopped. We all watched the surface. I pulled the rod back and back, trying quickly to regain the tension. I thought I'd lost it. Suddenly a big fish smashed through the water, spinning towards the boat like a firework. It dropped under the waves and ran for the far side of the loch. The line pulled tight, the rod bent hard over. Line fizzed off the spool. The fish ran and ran, then after about fifty yards it jumped high out of the water, and hung in the air.

'Oh shit, oh shit, oh shit, oh shit, oh shit. That's

a sea trout.' Duncan was at the motor pulling hard on the cord.

'Holy cow. Do you think so?' The fish was huge.

Richard wrinkled his nose. 'Don't know about that, Duncan. Looked like a salmon to me. A bit of a kipper.'

'Kipper my arse. Bloody sea trout. Salmon wouldn't jump about like that. Salmon would sulk on the bottom. That's a sea trout. It must be. Hold on to it, Charlie! Don't lose it! That's the fish of a lifetime!'

After three pulls at the motor cord he gave up, clattered towards the oars, and rowed hard upwind. The fish didn't show again. It ran deep, and as Duncan rowed I won back line, pumping the rod until we were above the fish. Slowly it came up. The broad back broke the surface and she was there, the gills stroking in and out.

'That's a salmon all right. Stale old girl too,' said Richard, pleased to be right.

'Bollocks,' said Duncan, scooping at her with a net. He missed, and nearly fell in. 'It's a big fish, that. Even so, it's a big salmon. For here anyway.' He was grunting and panting as he lifted her in. 'That'll be the biggest salmon this year, I'm sure,' he said. 'Twelve pounds, I reckon. Shame though. 'Twould have been one hell of a sea trout.'

I didn't say anything. I felt like I'd lost the fish a hundred yards out.

Richard looked at the two of us. 'Salmon's a salmon, lads.'

Over lunch in the fishermen's shed beside the loch, a square box of wood with ropes slung over the top to hold it down in a wind, we sat and talked, and ate bread rolls smeared with the Primula cheese out of a tube. Richard was feeling upbeat after we'd caught a salmon so quickly. 'We'll try a few of those drifts again this afternoon,' he said. 'Must be more fish about. This is looking good, Chuck!'

But the afternoon was slow. Nothing happened. Clouds lifted, and gave way to blue sky. In the evening sunlight caught the shallow hills, and out to the west across the sea we could see two rainbows. But it was bright over the island, the fish stayed down, and we cast over and over until the salmon of the morning became an unsure memory, and we felt that the loch was probably empty.

The next day we passed the house on the crossroads on the way to a new loch. Duncan saw washing on the line, and sang in a half-whisper to himself, 'Big white knickies, under lily-white titties. Oh yes. Oh yes. Ha ha.' Then he fell silent for a few minutes. 'Must be a long winter,' said Richard, chuckling. Duncan didn't hear him.

That day we caught nothing, and Duncan's tide of jokes ebbed as the hours wore on. It was cold. Urgent squalls blew in from the Atlantic. You could see them approach across the water, sometimes even hear them coming, a grey thresher drawing across the water. Rain leaked down inside our coats and ached every joint with cold. Mid-afternoon I looked at my right finger, puffed white with damp and red across the inside of the first knuckle from the draw of the wet line. Two fish turned at us, and Richard had one solid pull he was sure came from a salmon. He was just starting to get depressed when it happened, and it seemed to make him worse.

'These fish are as bored as I am. We need to wake them up.' I sat up and looked through my tackle bag for the tin of lures I use when the rainbow trout at Blagdon are chasing fish fry, and took out a two-inch white Mazuka.

'You'll nae use that fockin' thing on this loch.' Duncan folded his arms.

'Come on, Duncan, it's what they eat at sea. It'll cheer them up.' I bit off the Goat's Toe, tied on the lure, and threw it out across the waves. It was dry, and fluffy, and bobbed on the surface like a fledgling chicken, the brightest spot in a dark landscape.

'Och, for fock's sake,' said Duncan. In the context of his foul jokes and innuendoes this took me by surprise. I was starting to warm to Duncan.

'Bet you a pint that fly catches a sea trout.'

'I don't drink.'

The fly sat there, absurd, like his fantastical knickers. Too proud to give up, I pulled the fly back through the water, and cast again. Even at a distance we could see the tail wiggle through the waves. On the third cast a silver fish turned at it.

'Did you see that? Told you. This fly never fails.' Duncan turned to look the other way, like I was torturing his dog. I glanced at Richard, who shook his head gently.

'Well, the Goat's Toe took the salmon, so let's stick to it, hey?' I wound up, and bit off the soggy Mazuka. The Mazuka killed the day. Duncan didn't bother with any more jokes, and the loch was useless anyway. On the way home he only groaned inwardly as we passed the crossroads, no comment about knickers or white titties. We dropped him at the gate to his bungalow. He walked up the drive without saying good-night. I asked Richard if he thought I'd offended Duncan. Richard thought I had, but that Duncan would get over it. We drove the rest of the way without speaking, each thinking about the spectral sea trout, and our strange boatman. I looked out to the west. Another glorious sky hanging over a burnt car.

The days rolled on like this.

Loch fishing has a rhythm that can entrance or imprison you, and the division between the two is blurred. We drifted without a strike, and moved with every drift across that blurred division, until Richard, who for the last half-day had gone into a catatonic state in the stern, looked up and suggested he'd rather shut his old chap in a door than stay in this boat any more, and why didn't we go for a little drive? Duncan turned the boat around, saying he was sorry the sea trout weren't here, that it really was better than this most of the time. He showed us around the island, and told stories, and groaned each time we passed the crossroads. Once the lady was in the garden, and the words came whistling out as if Duncan was a kettle on the stove.

'Ooooh. Look at that . . . for fock's sake. Oooooh. Oooooh. Little titties. Look at them. Little white buns. Ha ha. You'll nae be needing that berassiere when I come and visit yer!'

We collared a guy with a small boat in the harbour, and he took us fishing for mackerel the following morning. It was something to get the rod bent. We came home with a bucketful, and Jim the fishery manager bit his pipe again. Duncan was pleased with the day off, but Jim's mood changed visibly each time we returned having not fished properly. For Jim it wasn't good enough to give up on the dream – we had to search every corner until we found fragments of it, and then arrange those fragments into at least a resemblance of what ought to be. Maybe he was right.

I fished alone on the last day, looking for fragments. Richard stayed in and watched golf on the telly.

Bruce, a regular who drank with Jim, was in the hall when I came in that evening, studying the book of catch returns. 'Good evening,' he said. 'Jim's written up the book, and your fish is in it.'

'Those fish on the tiles yours?' asked Richard, feigning idle interest. I looked at the book, saw my fish, its weight marked up a little, and below that a string of three sea trout to Bruce's name. 'Three? Well done. How did you catch them?'

'On a small fly of my own. Nothing special. I did work for them, though. I hear you gave up. Watched the golf.'

Richard was in the doorway. He shrugged at Bruce, who turned away. Richard looked again to check Bruce couldn't see, and then pulled a face at the fish. After Bruce walked away he called me over. 'Take a look,' he said. 'And tell me if they are sea trout.' There were three fish on the slab, one a perfect sea trout, square tailed, and hard, like a wild fish. The two bigger fish had scars, missing scales and worn-out fins. I picked one up at the tail. 'If that's a sea trout,' whispered Richard, 'I'm Batman. Are they in the book as sea trout?' I told him they were. 'Well that's it then.' Richard was delighted. 'We've cracked it. Half the bloody fish here are escaped farmed salmon. Let's take a scale. We'll get them checked at Pitlochry. I'll eat my hat if that's a wild fish. God, I'd love to know. It'll be the best thing to come out of the trip.' He picked scales off each fish, and flicked them into the corner of my fly box.

Jim was in the bar. 'Watched golf this afternoon, then?' he asked Richard.

'Yes I'm afraid I gave up. No good. No staying power. Back of the class.'

Jim puffed smoke through tight lips. 'You'll nae catch them in front of a bloody telly, that's for sure.'

Richard told him we'd seen Bruce's fish, that Bruce must have the knack. Jim said that Bruce knew how to work the water, knew it wasn't a holiday camp. Richard then asked if farmed fish ever got up into the sea trout systems. One or two maybe, replied Jim, not so you'd notice. Richard mentioned that the fish farmer he'd met earlier that day had seen a salmon jumping in the effluent tank of his smolt-rearing shed. There was a long silence, and then Jim said, 'Well, you boys will be off this evening, then.' Yes we would, we said, heading home, sorry to go. 'Aye,' said Jim.

We moved to the corner of the bar with our beers, looking through the window at the red and orange lights of the ferry as it docked. The lights were distorted by rain dripping down the glass. Duncan walked over from the bar, and asked if he could buy us a drink. Richard said that we'd buy him one.

'Just a coffee, thanks,' said Duncan.

'Thanks, Duncan,' I said, shaking his hand. 'We've enjoyed your company. The fishing was shite, but the jokes were great.'

'Ah well, sorry about the fishing, lads. It was slow all right. Next year. You must come again?'

I stood on the deck with Richard, and watched the hotel windows as the ferry pulled away. 'Thank crap that is one place I will never see again. Not in this life anyway,' Richard said, leaning back on the handrail. 'Got those scales?'

I said I had.

'Chuck 'em over the side.'

We walked inside to fall asleep on the cool vinyl of the bar seats, the sound of the engine vibrating through the boat.

Somewhere Else

THIS GREY, RAIN-STREAKED CLOUD BANK MOOCHED like a wet dog across the bed of chalk that runs the length of the country between where I live and the south-west. Everyone was talking about the weather, and about the mayfly hatch that just wasn't quite happening – according to the calendar it should have been over by now – and asking whether that was it, or whether it was still to come. Tony and Ronnie can be relied on for good reports. I rang them one after the other. Tony had seen a few mayfly hatch on the River Piddle; Ronnie had one good afternoon on the Frome. 'That can't be it,' said Tony. Ronnie said that it was a funny year for sure.

Late one morning the cloud broke, and I drove south across the Fens, heading for a particular bend in a river two hundred and fifty miles and five hours away. It was the first leg of a circular trip that I had more or less planned, though parts of it had been left deliberately vague to accommodate things like days of grey weather. Along the road I watched the sky – it's hard not to on the Fens – the tracer lines of cirrus clouds riding from one horizon to the next, the mirrored geometry of fenland drains. Looking at that expressionless order is like staring out to sea or across a lake.

Skies in the south-west are closed in by comparison, but this one particular bend is in a landscape just like the Fens. The river has run off its steep hills. The gradient has melted away. All the side streams run in where the hills are packed close together, like folds in a blanket, then suddenly the folds peel away north and south, leaving a flat plain a mile wide. Pylons stretch across the land, and hedgerows break the monotonous flatness. The road and railways have turned away with the hills, and it is quiet. You'll see sparrowhawks, hares, red deer. Upstream a tumour on the hill marks an ancient burial ground. Just nearby is the ghost of a drunk horseman.

I'd seen a fish at the bend earlier in the year when I was down with Patrick. We'd crossed the field.

'It's always worth a look,' I told him. 'Not much there, but if there is it could be big.'

It was windy. It usually is down here. A few small olives were struggling to get off the surface. We stared at the featureless corner, and Patrick was doubtful. 'Let's get back to the carrier,' he said. 'We know they're taking over there.' I said we should give it a minute. Downstream a fish dimpled the surface. Once. Then again a while after. It was coming up slowly, and only occasionally, like it had forgotten to feed and then suddenly remembered again. It could have been any size.

With a shrug of the shoulders we decided to have a go. We slid into the river, crossed a long way upstream, and she stopped rising. Just like that. We went off to fish elsewhere – it was Patrick's last day. I knew I'd come back on my own.

Some fish can only be caught when you're alone, and there was something about that place. I'd watched it for years, I'd waded through the middle of the stream, run my feet across the corrugated furrows of the river bed; scars a quarter of a century old, left by the draglines which turned a stream into a canal. On the river bank I'd found the piles of rounded flint, and gravel stacked high against tree roots, and planned how to put it all back. To catch and touch a wild trout down here is not the same as catching a trout in a river where there are lots of them. It's against the odds and it gives a sense that nature can overcome. As often as not nowadays, I go fishing in search of that feeling, as much as I go fishing for fish.

This time there was no hurry. I had all evening. I strung up the rod as I walked along the track, and sixty yards downstream – taking no chances – I waded to the far side, and then slowly upriver, waiting for each ripple to die away before I made the next step. It was warm. A few spent mayflies sailed along the far edge. I stood still against the reeds, the only sound the water curling around my legs. Then *balloop*. I waited five minutes for the next rise – the surface was quiet again. I planned to cast once to each rise, then wait – the only way I'd know I had-n't put the fish down.

It took three casts, and for that quarter-hour I still wasn't sure how large the trout was. The fly van-ished in a delicate swirl. I paused, then lifted the rod, but only so far. The weight at the end of the line was still, and solid. The surface ballooned, then fell quiet. The bend in the rod held steady, then suddenly dropped. Six feet away from the swirling ripple a trout jumped out of the river and fizzed towards me, half in half over the water, the tail skipping the sur-face. Then heading the thirty feet back to where she'd taken the fly, she ran so hard that she slid up the far bank, up on to the mud. I could see the brown flanks, and the depth of the body. She held on the edge for a moment, as if stunned, gasping, then flipped her body awkwardly and slipped back into the water. Now she swam fast downriver, right past my legs, her tail beating so fast I heard the vibra-tions, like the sound of a muffled propeller. I moved just in time. The fly line curled upriver, though the fish was now below me, moving quickly.

I caught up with her exactly where I'd walked into the river thirty minutes before. She was a light olive, with black spots as dense as the spots on a leopard, and only a few small red ones, all along the dorsal line. She was deep, really deep. I held four fingers under her belly, and the dorsal fin was level with my outstretched thumb. Getting on for the shape of a perch, she must have weighed at least four pounds. The hook fell out of the roof of the mouth. I grabbed a picture, then held her in the water, just for a moment, until I felt the strength in her. Then she swam away.

One day I'll get round to mending the stream here, though heaven knows when. I've moved away now and the place grows more remote each year. We fixed a stretch upriver a few years back, when I lived here. We scraped the gravel off the bank, and placed it back in long riffles. Sticking plaster, really. The lady who owns that piece of stream can remember the water board arriving with diggers, the scar of gravel they left piled along the bank. She remembers that the engineers told her husband it would improve the fishing. What it did was break his heart. It wasn't the same again. A living river changes, a constant process. Erosion here, deposition there. And like this it will fix itself in time. But it's possible, if you have no soul, to kill a river, or as good as kill it. You can crack it open and pull out the spine, and leave it limp and helpless to move. Those water engineers sucked the marrow out of it.

I sat there on the bank and thought about holding the bastards under until the bubbles stopped. It's not good to get so angry. We have to work with them now. Run conservation applications past them for approval. If I were in charge they'd put it all back, piece by piece, with their teeth.

I didn't cast any more that evening. I'd driven two hundred and fifty miles to cast only three times. But I'd given myself an annual fix, confirming again what I knew already. In all the ways I could think of, the fishing day was over. Those three casts were enough. Now I pointed the Land Rover north again, another long drive to another bend in another river. This river marks itself down in my mind for a different set of reasons. Certainly not because it signifies some potent flicker of hope in a beleaguered world – although I suppose everywhere wild trout swim does that in some way – more because the place is slightly unreal.

The pool has an oriental name. A steel bridge of Victorian extravagance crosses the lower end, where the water slides over bright rocks to a waterfall. Both banks are lined with tall trees, deciduous and ever-green, and the banks climb steeply away. The light is always a dull, watery blue. When it is misty, and it often is, the trees disappear and reappear in a way that divorces them from the land. Sound is chan-nelled down the passage of the river, muffled and intensified at the same time – so that you can hear clearly that someone beyond sight is talking, but not exactly what they are saying. The water seems to sigh towards you, coiling like some frigid laval flow. When I fish this river I feel that I am fishing in a world slightly removed from our own – that beneath the hard rocks under my feet there is a band of air. I feel like I'm fishing in a Chinese watercolour.

Mark was on a tight schedule. He always is. There's a reluctance in his voice when you first call up and put to him the idea of going fishing, and that reluctance is driven by the inevitability of his decision to join you, and leave his desk behind. His desk is a casualty of where he lives, and of the reasonably legitimate idea that it is part of Mark's work – he's a fishing writer – to walk out of his house and go fishing. Mark can see trout rising from his desk, and frankly it's amazing he gets anything else done.

So the official line was that I should ring Mark when I got close, and he'd see if he could make it, and the unwritten script was that if I arrived at the right time – late in the day after Mark had put in some time at the keyboard, and as the sun dipped under the tree line – he would definitely make it.

So I showed up at about five o'clock, and by six we were setting up beside the pool with the oriental name. It was another of those blue evenings, with a heaviness to the air that caused the olives that were hatching to sit on the water for some while drying their wings. A few trout were coming up intermittently to this thin hatch, and as usual the trick was to identify which of these was worth casting for. I can't remember who caught the first fish, only that for an hour or so Mark cast to the rippled water, and I to the flat run under the oak tree on the far bank, that we caught two or three trout in that time, and that the drag on the fly was as taxing as it normally is, that the trout seemed even fussier than usual. The lower end of the pool has a complexity to it that I find completely absorbing. And there are some huge trout under the oak tree, though I have yet to catch one. 'I could live at that end of the pool,' said Mark as I tried to think aloud about why I found it so compelling.

A few minutes after that a series of curses, agitated casts, and a heron-like intensity in Mark's stance crept in on my attention. Mark was attacking a problem that was evading me. I wandered up.

'What's going on?'

'Sedge are starting.' Mark said this with a level of assurance and excitement that showed he knew exactly what was going on, and exactly why that was a big deal.

'Here, fish this run, right at the top. The big fish have moved up to the shelf where the water spills in.'

He pointed to a thin run, where the stones showed clearly through six inches of water. I tied on a dry sedge, and on the first drift a brown back curled over the fly and tried to drown it. On the second or third I hooked into a powerful fish that ran straight to the head of the run and up across barely wet rocks, so that it pushed out a bow wave. Its beating tail threw up spray, as if it was some organic, intelligent torpedo. That fish was over a pound, and so was the second, hooked behind the same stone. After the third – a bigger fish – I felt ashamed of taking too many from the same run, but I cast again, more out of curiosity and disbelief than anything, and caught a fourth.

Mark had crossed to the far side, but he too thought the pool had had enough. He called over, 'Have you ever fished the run below the bridge?'

'Didn't know there was one.'

'There is, there is,' he said, and looked like he was about to let me in on a secret.

Below the bridge the river curls round in a long arc, the flow of water pressed against the far bank, a cliff of rock, where rhododendron bushes hang their branches in the water. We stepped down off the path to get a view of the run. Trout rose busily wherever we looked, and against the dying brightness over the hill upstream the air was thick with ephemeral spots of light – sedges tumbling from the water to the river bank.

For two hours we fished, both of us completely absorbed by this intense rise of trout. At last light I tried a few casts to a fish lying twenty yards downstream. He'd been going all evening, smacking sedges off the top, moving a lot of water. I hadn't got a good cast over him yet.

He was at the far point of a triangle created by the sill at the bottom of the pool. I was casting downstream across the sill, and the middle part of the cast kept sweeping away downriver, dragging the fly with it. But for once I got the fly close enough to his nose for him to grab it before the river did.

The trout scrapped around in the top pool for a few minutes and then, like a few others I'd caught that evening, swam over the sill. He felt heavy. The others had come round into the back eddy at my feet, but this one headed straight down, and with the weight of water behind him he unspooled a hundred yards of line before I could get to the far bank to chase him. I had to splash through thigh-deep water over slippery boulders and nearly fell.

As I clambered the far bank, eyes on the ground, and on the tip of the rod, which I was holding as high as I could, I almost walked right into a lad in chef's trousers. He was with a dog, a Staffordshire bull.

'Doin' it the hard way, eh?'

I looked at him, smiled and nodded. I was too busy to talk. The fish was big and I didn't want to lose him. The chef followed me down. He chatted away, though I wasn't interested until I'd got the fish in, so I didn't really hear what he was saying. Now my trout was ahead of me and still going, but I was gaining ground. I slackened the pressure on the line, and the trout settled in the edge of the pool he had reached. As I closed in I was careful not to tighten up too hard and make him run again.

At last I was below the fish. Now there was a chance that as I tightened he'd run upstream and play himself out. Instead he ran across, and around a boulder. The line caught on the edge of the rock. I heard the chef say 'Oh shit.' But it gave, slid over the top, and I was back with the fish. The tension in the line snapped across the stream, and the trout jumped. Really high, maybe two or three feet clear of the stream, back down with a heavy thump.

'Good one. Good one,' said my friend. It was the biggest I'd hooked up here. Over three pounds, and trout on this river play twice their weight.

I got it to the edge. It was a long but hard fish, its back as dark as a cupboard, khaki sides. The trout was tired out and I had to hold him in the current for some while. When finally he swam away I bit off the fly, and walked back up to find Mark. That was enough for the evening. The chef carried on downstream, said he'd see me around.

We made it back to the bar in time for a pint and sandwiches beside an inappropriately intense fire for a warm night in June. Wedding guests fell through doorways, singing loudly and out of tune. Mark and I were both coming round slowly, like patients waking from anaesthetic. We talked about all the good rivers hereabouts, and about how we'd never get to fish them all, and about what was so compelling about the place we'd just been.

'There's a guy I know. Lives on the lower part of this salmon river,' said Mark. 'And every spring he'll call me and say, "Hey there are March Browns hatching, and these big fish are just going silly." And I always say I'll be there in a few days. And I never go. Then a month later he'll call, and ask "Why are you never here for that hatch? You're a fool." And all I can say is "I'm never there because I'm always somewhere else."'

Up Annie's Creek

ABOUT TWO IN THE AFTERNOON, THE SUN BURNING like a spotlight inches from my neck, Dundee rounds the corner of Knife Island in his new boat. Ginny, his girlfriend, is with him. They see us, and cut back across the inlet. We've been all over the bay that morning, always ending up at this rock where we find a shoal of tiny trevally. We cast at them to feel fish on the line – we're looking for barramundi, but now anything will do.

'Hey Ronnie, they pull like hell, these little nutters.'

'GTs are the business. Street fighters. Always up for it.'

I'm into my fourth or fifth when Dundee cuts the engine. His wake slaps the side of our boat. The noise of water is loud in the silence. I turn round to greet them, bouncing up and down in the waves, my nine-weight fly rod hardly bent at all as the trevally swims in circles at the surface.

'Wotcha, guys,' says Dundee. 'Hey! You got something there?'

Ginny is sitting up on the foredeck in a Union Jack bikini, and she smiles, waiting for me to answer Dundee. She holds her hand up to shield the sun, and squints against the light. She lifts one knee, and her thighs slide open like scissors. She has fantastic brown thighs. I feel the sweat on my forehead.

'Oh this,' I say, suddenly feeling like I've been asked to take my pants down for a medical exam. 'This is nothing. We're just fooling around. It's so small.'

Dundee looks at the fish, nods, and turns to Grant, who is sitting by the wheel. 'Well, Grant, how's it goin'?'

'Slow, Dundee, slow. We ain't had nuthin'. Though we've had our shots, haven't we, lads?' There's forced optimism in Grant's voice. I know he's been talking with Dundee, in the evenings, those times he leaves Ronnie and me with our beers. A few seconds' silence is loaded with meaning.

'Guess so,' says Ronnie finally.

I'm trying to shake the baby GT loose when Dundee says matter-of-factly that they have had loads of pops from really big queenfish further out on the edge of the bay, and that Ginny who has hardly fished before hung a fifteen-pound queenfish on a fly rod. 'Pretty amazing, wasn't it, darling?' says Dundee.

'It was neat,' says Ginny.

'You should check it out, Grant,' says Dundee. 'You know the spot. There's big fish working out there.' With that Dundee thumbs his twin outboards back into life and says he has to get back quick to do some work on his trailer.

'Hell, I told him the spot to go to,' says Grant after they've gone. 'I told him the friggin' spot to go.'

Ronnie and I sit down and look at the water, thinking about the big queenfish, and our little trevally. The heat presses down like a hot engine block.

'Fantastic,' says Ronnie explosively. 'Fuckin' Croc Dundee comes over in his twenty-five-grand boat, with its oh so capacious casting deck, on which I'll bet my arse he's given Ginny more than fish to think about, and says she just caught a fifteen-pound queenie, though she's never been fishing before. And there's us standing there with two grands' worth of tackle and an eight-ounce GT to show for our troubles, feeling like kids on a pier. We supposed to be pleased for him or what?'

Grant shrugs, and suggests we go have a few casts somewhere else. He wants the fishing to come good, but he's also getting pissed off.

'We should have gone out there, fuck it,' he says suddenly. 'I always go out there on this day of the spectrum. That's where I go. I shouldn't have paid any attention to you guys wanting to fish the gutter by the dried out friggin' jellyfish. That's where I fish on days after the tide spectrum.'

I look at Ronnie and Ronnie says 'Perfect.'

It can go either way from here. I throw my fly

towards a mangrove bush, knowing I won't hook anything, and think about how I got to this point. I don't look for much from fishing or rather what I like about it is simple: the way the world shrinks to a connection with a creature whose life revolves around stuff like tides, weather, the phases of the moon. Making that connection is going to be difficult. If it were easy, it would be boring. But right now I'm too hot, pissed off and far from home to be so philosophical. Over the last couple of days there have been moments when I've thought fuck the mangrove swamps and wild beauty of the place, I need the violent pull of a large barramundi. Or, now the thought's occurred, Ginny's soft brown thighs. I'm clearly not going to get either.

This thing started back in Darwin. It was still dark. The heat of the night hit us as we dragged our bags through the revolving door and out of the air-conditioned foyer. Grant's pick-up was in the forecourt, his boat behind, under a plastic cover. Two days lost to aeroplanes, cable TV and Darwin's shopping malls, we were fidgety and keen to get going.

Driving through the outskirts of town and out into the night, the warm, salty air moved through the cab. Passing a sign to Alice Springs, over 1,200 kilometres away, it felt like the road would go straight there without turning a corner. Ronnie said that only a car journey lasting days would give a feeling for the vastness of Australia, but Grant shrugged his shoulders and said that after you've seen one piece of vastness, the rest is much the same. 'You guys hungry?' he asked later. It was quarter-past five. Inside the garage we ordered tea, and bacon and egg sandwiches taken from a pile, ready wrapped. I got the impression they were all for fishermen on their way out of the city: at the pumps outside stood two other trucks with fishing boats in tow. Grant nodded hello to a couple of guys.

Back on the road our thoughts ran ahead of the truck, mapping out the two weeks of fishing that waited for us at the end of all this flying and driving.

'What d'ya think, Grant?' asked Ronnie. 'Trophy barra's got to be twenty. We can catch a twenty. Trophy queenfish. What's a trophy queenfish? Fifteen?'

'There are some big ones out there all right,' said Grant.

We drove for another hour, before turning left on to a dirt track. Our headlights picked out a sign to Bynoe Bay. Beyond it light from the east slowly seeped over the horizon, picking out gaps in the trees. The bush, concealed in the darkness, filled out – at first the trees, then minute by minute the colours and shapes grew more precise, until the day had begun. Ahead of us a small kangaroo jumped across the weakening beam of the headlights. The rutted track turned a corner, past a grassy airstrip, and ahead of us stood a row of beach huts on stilts. Beyond them the sea.

We wasted little time getting on to the water – stopping only to chat with four guys who'd been out mining for jewfish at the bottom of deep holes in the bay. 'Shit,' said the fattest of them, 'I thought I was going over the side, that thing nearly pulled my arms out of their sockets. Hey, so far it's jewfish two, me, nil.'

The day was full of promise. We'd be fishing for all sorts: queenfish, Spanish mackerel, giant trevally, threadfin salmon – but mostly for barramundi, the real Aussie gamefish: an overgrown, psychopathic perch, with orange eyes set on the top of its head, and an upturned jaw. It hangs around swampy inlets, brackish and fresh water. But the saltwater barra is the prize – a silver and spectacularly airborne incarnation. As we motored out that first morning, running our fingers across the pink, orange and white lures we'd tied for the trip, wondering which to use first, Ronnie showed Grant a fly his daughter had tied for him – a mass of bright feathers. Grant shrugged. 'They'll have a go at anything,' he said. We liked this; we'd catch them till our arms ached. 'This is it, Charlie,' Ronnie shouted over the noise of the outboard. 'You've not caught fish till you beg for mercy and want to cut the line. This is where it happens.'

Bynoe Bay lies on the shoreline of the Northern Territories. Its estuaries fumble blindly inland amongst the mangrove swamps and sandy coves. The inlets turn and twist endlessly, are punctuated by islands, feed back on themselves. That morning we fished small bays, across headlands, in against the mangrove trees, while Grant chugged his boat along, shutting the throttle on and off, directing our casts, chatting keenly. Somehow though I felt I was still on my way to something – not exactly there yet.

The water was cloudy, and I'd expected it to be clear; we were casting blind, but I thought we'd see fish. And when the throttle blipped, the line bellied uselessly beside the boat, dragging the fly across the surface.

As we motored along, the sun rose in the sky, its fierce heat burning up our sweat. We stopped on the edge of a bay where a creek drained through the mangroves and waited for the barramundi that Grant told us would come out from amongst the tree roots as the tide fell. A dead jellyfish hung in the mangrove branches, like a piece of torn plastic. The swamp clicked with the sound of mud crabs. Then way back in the tangle of undergrowth I heard a sudden thump in the water. A ripple fanned out across the surface and through the trees.

'Hear that boofing noise? That's a barra,' whispered Grant.

It was quiet again. Then Grant pointed at something on the edge of the trees. 'That's a huge tail. See it? Really big. Shit, look at the size of it. Now cast right at him.' I couldn't see the fish.

'Right there,' he said. 'See that dark shape?'

'Thing that looks like a big leaf?' I asked.

'That's it, now cast right at it. No that's too far away, you've got to get it right on his nose. He's gotta see it. No! That's behind him.' The tail drifted off to the side, then vanished.

Occasionally the dusty silhouette of a fish would lift and show itself, and fade again into the brown water. We threw flies at every sign, but the flies were ignored. The tide was dropping quickly. Soon we could follow the shape of the creek on the exposed mudbank, and as the tide dropped further so the barra moved out of the trees and away into the bay. I saw their dark shapes move quietly past the boat. Suddenly a fish exploded on to Ronnie's fly, and was gone again. Grant began to worry about getting stuck on the mud, and we moved off, leaving a few bar-ramundi on the edge of the tree line drifting in and out of the sunlight. Ronnie and I watched the reced-ing scene, our fly lines trailing in the water as we backed away, feeling that the party was over; that we'd never got through the door.

It was midday, and mercilessly hot. We fished an hour or two longer for threadfin salmon as they boiled at the brown surface on the edge of the mud-flats, rounding up tiny prawns with their feelers. But the barra had disappeared, and the day lost shape. 'You sure these things take a fly, Grant?' asked Ronnie, after we'd run lures through the muddy soup a few hundred times.

Back at the camp I slept for hours, then in the early evening, as the light fell, I found Ronnie tying

Bimini twists on the veranda of our beach hut. Three days away from home, we were keen to find out the journey had been worth it.

'That was a strange day,' I said.

'I don't get it,' said Ronnie. 'We were out there for seven hours, but in all honesty we had a good shot at those barra for an hour. No, fifty minutes tops. The rest was a boat ride. I'm feeling a bit deflated here, Charlie. I mean, was that it? I can't believe that was it.'

The next day turned out the same way. Barramundi drifted in and out of sight, across shafts of sunlight, like sick dogs looking for shade. Then out of nowhere one fish turned on me, jarring my rod so hard that the fly sprung back through the air to the edge of our boat. But the tide had already seeped back into the creek, and I could see mud beneath us through the dusky water. 'Better get outta here,' said Grant. By noon the day fractured beneath the weight of the heat.

'Hey, don't judge this fishing by what you're seeing at the moment.' Grant found us deep in thought, leaning against the bar. 'It's the end of a tide spectrum. Water's big and fast. The fish don't feed well now.' He paused for a moment, watching our faces. 'Wait till we get to the billabong. That place is crawling with fish. Then we'll be back here for the next spectrum, the seven days leading up to the new moon. Hell, these days were only ever a warm-up.'

Ronnie shrugged. The trip needed nothing more than a few good fish, and they would come.

We woke at four and drank our coffee in the dark, too tired to talk. It was warm on the veranda, and across Bynoe Bay I could see the faintest orange glow above the tree line. I thought about how we rewrite each day with expectation. I sometimes wonder if I'm obsessive or unrealistically optimistic, yet every fisherman does the same. But it's impossible to fully erase the memory of failure too – and the memory can be cumulative. Everyone has a breaking point. The others were ready to go. I didn't need to worry about that right now.

We jumped into the truck as the first light wicked up the blotting paper sky. An hour later, when Grant cut the boat engine in a musty corner of the Finniss River, the sun wasn't yet above the trees, though the sky was now a weak and distant blue. It was quiet, but slowly the jungle came to life around us – whooping bird calls, and the ratcheting of frogs, at first far off and occasional, until the noise was close and all around. Suddenly Ronnie was into a tarpon. The fish sliced up through the dark water and broke through the surface. It bounced across the water like oil across a hot pan, touching down only to jump again. Finally by the boat it shook madly on the end of the line. I took a picture of this fish, its silver head slotted together like shiny armour plating – a scale model of the Caribbean monsters, it weighed only two pounds, but it had pulled Ronnie's trout rod into a barrel hoop.

They were everywhere, slashing at every cast. That instant one was on my line too, jumping all over the river. 'This is bloody brilliant,' I shouted. 'Real fish actually taking the fly.' The electric thrill of a live rod was enough. We brought a dozen or more to the boat, until at last in a shady hole Ronnie broke his fly off on something he described as 'a lot fuckin' bigger than those tarpon'.

'That was a barra,' said Grant softly.

'Try a popper,' he said. 'Throw it up that side channel as far you can, right in under the trees.' We were anchored at the outlet to a mazy creek overhung with trees and vines. Fifty yards upriver the water surface heaved gently, and the head of a crocodile turned slowly towards us like a compass needle. 'Don't fall in,' he added.

Ronnie threw his popper close up against a floating mass of weeds and sticks, and brought it back with quick stabs on the line. The fly made a loud glooping noise as it dived and surfaced pulling a trail of bubbles behind it. The water erupted. 'Magic,' whispered Ronnie as he strained against the sudden weight on the line. 'Slow it, slow it,' urged Grant. But the line went solid. Ronnie pulled against a dead weight, shook his head despondently and bent the rod over until the line came free.

The rod jumped in his hand.

'He's still on. He's good. He's pulling,' Ronnie exclaimed.

We saw the copper, Morse code flashes of a fish spinning against the line, deep under the boat. Grant leant down over the side, grabbing the tail as soon as the fish broke the surface, and swung the barra aboard in a mess of water, scales and strands of weed. The fish lay gasping on the blue matting, its menacing eyes now stupid and helpless. Ronnie pushed his hat back and wiped his forehead.

'Thank God we've got that out the way. A fish, hey? Well done, pal,' he said, shaking Grant's hand.

'Got another popper, Ronnie?' I asked. 'Don't need a popper,' said Grant. 'These guys'll hit at anything. Let's go downstream.'

We fished as the boat drifted on the current, and caught barramundi, sooty grunter, archer fish. Ronnie did better than me, and I asked again after a popper. 'Don't need a popper,' said Grant. The sun was overhead now, burning straight down between the trees, and the day changed. The jungle was quiet again, as though the heat had rolled in a blanket of silence, and the air was still, and oppressive. The river too was quiet, and there came a moment when we knew nothing would take. We ate lunch under the trees, with cold flannels on our heads. 'Let's shoot pool,' said Grant. 'There's a bar near here. Hey, the barmaid's a real looker. You gotta check her out. Used to be Miss Australia.' Ronnie looked over and shrugged. I nodded. It was too hot to speak.

*　　*　　*

She had a face like an angry warthog. It was an out-back pub – a sheet-iron single-storey building, and out front a dusty forecourt surrounded by plants in whitewashed barrels – a forlorn effort at domestication in the face of the shimmering jungle which began at the back door. Inside, the TV was on quietly in the corner, tuned to Aussie football. Behind the bar a wiry old man sat on a bar stool. He turned to us when we came in, blinked like there was dust in his eye, shouted something towards the kitchen and turned back to the football. I looked around, noticing the vast, stuffed barramundi above the TV, and by the door a few shelves dedicated to the essentials of outback life – tinned food, plasters, batteries. Ronnie set up the pool table while I waited at the bar. A woman appeared, arms folded, in the doorway, and asked me what I wanted. 'Three Cokes please,' I said, glancing at Grant who was trying not to laugh.

Grant pointed out a picture by the door. 'Fished this bugger out of the Finniss – where you just been,' he said. A hand in a surgical glove pulled something from the entrails of a crocodile. Wedged inside were the head, arms and torso of a person. The old man noticed, and turned from his TV, cracking a grin that revealed only three front teeth.

The picture stuck in my mind during our days at Corroboree billabong – at one point four crocodiles watched us from the muddy hollows of a bay. We cast our flies right at them, into the tangles of lily stems and festering algae soup, hunting sarratoga. The crocs hardly moved but even so we pissed over the side with an unusual degree of caution. Grant terrified us with stories of drunk idiots who'd ended their days as crocodile shit.

The sarratoga were as surprising as fish get – a fat, snake-like body, with three powerful fins at the back. They'd lie in the shallows, under lily pads, or in tangles of rotting sticks and weed at the water's edge, waiting for frogs or mice or little fish. We used poppers with heavy weed-guards, casting right into the snags.

'How far in?' I asked Grant.

'All the way to the bank.' This was exactly the sort of snag I'd spent my fly-fishing days learning to avoid. I pulled the fly as slowly as I could to clear the hard stems, then in a clear patch two feet across, yanked the popper twice. Now the fly was right up against a raft of lily pads. I gingered the fly on to the lilies. 'Easy, Charlie,' said Grant. 'When you get it to the edge plop that fly in like it's a frog.'

Sarratoga follow the slow passage of a fly through the undergrowth, then suddenly attack. You have to heave them away from the thicket double quick. The fly vanished in a swirl of water as soon as it fell off the lily pad. My fly rod wrenched forwards, and I was leaning back against something of prehistoric strength. 'Better get him outta there,' said Grant. Odds are stacked the sarratoga's way. If he gets you round a lily stem, you're smoked.

I pulled at the fish like I was trying to dock a barge, and eventually it gave. You'd think this fantastic inhabitant of bogs would be lost in the open water, that its fins would be in the wrong place, but once into the wide channel of the billabong, a large sarratoga will tussle you all the way in.

Grant had my fish by the tail. 'Hey, Charlie,' he said. 'This one's a hooter.' We posed it by a lily flower, its handsome head in pearly copper, an upturned mouth, and goatee beard; like an anaconda swallowing Ezra Pound feet first. We caught a lot of them.

The days at Corroboree eased the unhappy time at Bynoe into a half-formed memory. The billabong was busy in the cool of the morning. Egret, jabiru and ibis stalked the margins; tarpon splashed the water like the trailing rain of a thunderstorm. A solitary tree heavy with blossom burst into the air – the blossom a flock of white parakeets. At night we shot pool at the local motel, and slept in air-conditioned cargo containers. Each naked light bulb was the epicentre of a food chain. I got the idea the place moved on the backs of restless insects.

Grant took us to Humpty Doo's tavern. 'Used to be a rough old place,' he said as we drove in through the chain-link perimeter fence. 'Had a reputation for fighting. If a fight kicked off, the police would lock the gates and hose the place down.' It looked rough now. Harleys and custom bikes ticked in the sun out front. Their owners shot pool in the shade. Two had shaven heads, three had beards like Old Moses. All six wore torn jeans, work boots and mucky white vests. My aqua blue Columbia bonefish shirt might as well have read AUSSIE BIKERS SQUAT TO PISS.

To make things worse, the only girl in the place was playing pool in Daisy Duke shorts and the cue ball kept finding its way to our side of the table. I've never tried so hard not to look at an arse. 'Even think about it and someone will park a Harley down your throat,' agreed Ronnie.

We thought about fishing instead. The billabong was great, but we were here to catch saltwater barra. We analysed the tide patterns, their subtle variations in the six days leading up to the new moon; how we'd target queenfish one day, barra the next. It was time to head back to Bynoe. We were ready to believe that the good times would roll. We didn't know they were already behind us.

Bynoe is exactly the frigging same. We motor hard from point to point, and in between chug along the mangrove margins throwing an investigative cast here and there, until we settle for the spot by the dried-out jellyfish. Barramundi drift out of the trees like zombies in a B-movie. I take one maniac smash on the line. Gone as quickly as it came. When Grant starts the outboard, and says 'Gotta get outta here boys' my heart sinks. I am in a boat on the River Styx. I am chained to a rock, and barramundi eat my heart. Three days into the second Bynoe leg, and it's like we never left the place, and the billabong was a mirage. We try to forget the failure, but optimism can defy gravity for only so long. The days bleed away from us.

In the end the baby trevally are at least something. They hit the fly, they bend the rod. They add shame to despondency. The reservoir of memory fills quickly, until the point when Dundee tells us about Ginny's fish, and all at once I am over the edge. Each cast is no longer an opportunity to touch the wild heart of the outback. Each cast is pure futility. Sometimes it hurts to stand and unhook the fly from the stripping guide.

Through will rather than instinct, it is possible to look at the sunrise and muster a veneer of hope. The day after Ginny's triumph we rise early and hunt for barra at first light. We even find some on the mudflats, though they are spooky and uninterested, and we chase them for nearly two hours without a take. Then we run up to Turtle Island, where Dundee and Ginny caught their queenfish. Dundee is already there with two clients from Sydney pulling up queenies easily on spinning equipment. They've caught five. Gulls are busting into the water, and we see the slashing spray below them. But the shoals move quickly, and I just can't strip the fly fast enough. Finally it becomes obvious we should troll, teasing up the fish with a hookless plug towed out the back. None of us thinks this is fly-fishing, but Ronnie says we should get a queenfish on the line before we make up our minds. Suddenly one appears, thumping the plug, coming in again and again until Ronnie's rod snaps over. 'Into one, Ronnie?' asks Grant. He doesn't answer, just stares at the sea where the queenfish leaps and runs. When we get it aboard, its flanks yellow with adrenalin, Grant says he is glad to get a monkey off his back. I catch one too and he says let's go and do some proper fishing.

Six hours later we have a small flathead to show for our high-mindedness. Tomorrow will always be better. Grant says that anything is possible. 'Yeah,' says Ronnie. 'I know. The Queen Mum could appear on that rock over there and pour us all a Pimm's. What I'm trying to get my head around here is likelihood.' In the evening he says, 'Put it like this. Casting into muddy soup all day long when the chances of catching something range from extremely unlikely to fuck all, is not what you call fly-fishing.'

'How can you call this magnificent place shite?' asks Grant. Later I chat to Ronnie. We decide between us to leave off the pressure and fish as positively as we can. 'Let's just see if the fat lady sings, shall we?'

Two days left and we have the perfect tide. We catch a small threadfin, and a couple of tiny catfish. At Knife Island Ronnie hands Grant his rod and says, 'You catch one.' It's getting dark, and I'm on the nose of the boat trying to cast further than Grant – his

comments have pissed me off, and it gives me something to focus on. I'm getting the timing right this
evening, casting a heavy popper and thirty yards of
fly line, and when the tippet folds over I notice the
first few inches of backing in my left hand. Suddenly
a fish hits my fly, and whips the rod round. It's way
out under the mangrove trees, and jumping like crazy
in the blue light of evening. The moon is up over the
trees of Knife Island. The barramundi tail-walks the
water, then surges for the shelter of the mangroves.
The spinning reel handle raps my knuckles.

Very little is said about this barramundi. It is long
and silver and seems to glow in the half-light. I ease
it back. Ronnie is quiet. Grant and I shake hands,
and we put in a few more casts before heading in.
But it's impossible to believe things will change. In
fact this solitary barramundi just accelerates the sense
of futility we were giving in to. Fate tortures despair
with hope.

Ronnie wakes the next day, and the moonlight
barramundi is a mirage. 'This is hell,' he says.
'Torture. I'd rather suffer the ravages of syphilis; have
my toenails pulled out; go to the dentist to have all
my teeth drilled. Not one of those stink holes has
produced a fish, not one. We've cast flies into that
putrefied algae soup for hours a day, for not one
solitary fish.'

Unsurprisingly, Grant is spending more time in the
bar with Dundee and the other guides, less with us.
When he comes to see us it is hard not to talk about

the fishing, and when we do that we get depressed. I've seen the other guides turn and look our way. Ronnie carries his mood to the boat, and half-way to Knife Island Grant tells him not to get angry.

'You haven't seen me angry, pal, and you wouldn't want to,' says Ronnie.

'You even dream of getting angry with me,' says Grant. 'You'll want to wake up and apologise.'

I notice a few fish hitting the water fifty yards behind us, and point it out to lighten the air. Grant starts to back out to them, and Ronnie says, 'I've been telling him that all week, Chaz. That's where the fish are hitting, but he's been telling me I'm talking rubbish.'

It quietens down for a while. Then Grant says we are whingeing poms and that all the other guides think we are arseholes. This proves the last straw for Ronnie, who points out that he is a Scot, not a pom, before resigning himself to the misery.

It's another perfect barramundi tide – muddy water and a few shots at spectral fish, which are not hungry. We're arguing more and more with Grant, and Ronnie is really depressed. To lighten things I draw up a list of the species we have caught: grinner, flattie, catfish, threadfin, snapper, golden snapper, bream, longtong, mackerel – all small; mudcrab in a crab trap; two good queenfish; one example of the quarry, a saltwater barramundi.

'Can't put the barra on my list,' says Ronnie proudly. 'I haven't caught one.'

* * *

Up Annie's Creek

On the morning of our last day I feel the poetry of the trip will be more complete if we catch nothing. We've only a few hours and Grant tells us we're going up to a place called Annie's Creek. Ronnie and I joke on the boat ride up there: 'Will the fat lady sing? Will that fat lady sing at Annie's Creek? The crowds are packing the theatre. The orchestra is tuning up. But will the fat lady sing?' And fuck it all, she croaked out a note. We found barramundi in clear water, and a few of them turned at the fly. Ronnie caught one too. I've never seen him look so glum.

I've Got Gloves

'ARE Y'ALL GOING TO SASKATCHATOON TOO?'

I turned round. She was talking to me.

'I think so,' I said, 'but isn't it just called Saskatoon?'

She looked away distracted, as though she hadn't heard. I shrugged and went back to my book.

'I'm worried we'll miss the plane,' she said, a minute later. I looked at her. She was wearing jeans, a buckled belt with rodeo scene, crocodile boots, a spangled shirt. She fidgeted with her bag, strained to look out the window, then waved to catch the eye of the stewardess – our plane from Butte to Vancouver was circling endlessly above the city. 'Are we going to make that?' she asked, pointing at a line on a travel itinerary. The stewardess shrugged her shoulders, without troubling to look.

'They're on strike down there.'

Behind time we hurried through Vancouver airport. I offered to carry her case, so we could move more quickly. By now it would have been rude to

leave her to struggle. We missed the Calgary connection, caught the next an hour later, then missed
the first Saskatoon flight by ten minutes. It was an
awkward moment as we looked round the departure lounge for a place to sit and ended up side by
side. She was into horses, and was heading to a
horse show in Saskatoon – 'Saskatchatoon' as she
kept saying. I tried again to correct her, but she
wasn't hearing me. She was still talking about
horses. At last we got to the gate, and the lady
asked the steward as he checked her ticket, 'Is this
the plane to Saskatchatoon?' I could see his eyebrow rise, though he didn't look up from the ticket.
Then as he handed it back he said, 'Ma'am, you
have combined the province and the town most ele-
gantly.' She didn't seem to hear him either – just
took her ticket back, and walked quickly down the
gangway.

I thought that might be the last I saw of her, but
as I waited for my bags in the small terminal at
Saskatoon she came up from behind and asked in a
cheery way, 'So, where are y'all from?' I told her I
was from England. She paused, a little surprised.
Head to one side she said, 'You speak real good
English for a foreigner.' She smiled. 'Thanks,' I said.
'Er . . . the English do speak quite good English.' I
said it as gently as I could, wondering if she'd hear
me this time. She stopped, and blushed. 'Of course
. . . of course. Oh.' Without saying anything else she
walked away through the exit gate, under a poster

of a smiling angler holding up a gigantic pike. The gigantic pike was why I was here.

In Saskatoon I met up with Kathy, a tourism officer for the state who had been sent to look after me for the week. I didn't need looking after, so this bothered me. I was worried that she'd get bored with fishing. If she got bored I'd feel bad, relent and end up looking at the sorts of things tourist officers think magazine writers want to look at. Ethnic crap, big hills. I explained that I wasn't really interested in any of the wonderful things the state had to offer, other than catching gigantic pike. Kathy looked relieved. She said there wasn't much else to look at on Lake Athabasca, other than pike. Uranium City was the nearest town, and there wasn't much to see there. Besides, she was looking forward to her first ever fishing trip. It would get her out of the office for a week. Kathy took me out to dinner at an Italian restaurant in downtown Saskatoon. The hotel guidebook said the place was a pretty provincial town, no comma after pretty.

We flew north catching glimpses through the cloud of field patterns, but these broke up into patches of woodland and scrub, then unbroken forest and water for mile after mile. Stony Rapids is a small town on the far eastern tip of Lake Athabasca, an outpost.

I stood on the airstrip, breathing in the scent of forest and dust. One or two light planes flew in and out while we were there, and the far-off drone of engines underlined the quiet. Other noises – trucks, chainsaws – came in on the wind from a long way off in the woods, and the planes could be heard long before they were seen.

An old yellow school bus took us from the airstrip to the dock, its engine rattling like flint in a tin can, spitting black smoke out into the clean air. I sat on the bench-seat, and looked out through a cracked window as we passed rows of wooden houses and rubbish bins along the edge of the dusty road.

At the dock two float planes rocked on the water, catching the afternoon sun. To the right a sandy road curled out of sight over a hill, and once in a while as we waited a truck would ride over the top, a plume of dust following the rumble of tyres. We sat on our bags listening to the water lapping against the floats. Stella, Cliff's wife was already there with a week's supplies for the camp. Stella and Kathy chatted a while, but the peace of the place was infectious. The talk dried up. I closed my eyes against the sun, and let the lapping water and the drone of engines soothe my busy head.

One or two float planes passed over and once I asked Stella if the plane was Cliff's. She shook her head. A while later a sharper, barking sound came in low, and from a long way out over the trees. 'That's Cliff,' she said. I stood up. For a minute maybe two the plane closed in, still out of sight. Then all of a sudden Cliff came in shaving the tree line. The plane hit the lake, throwing water spray high in the air. For a moment it vaporised in a burst of light.

'Shiny plane.'

'Needs a clean. Cliff'll polish it up end of season.'

The plane drew alongside. Cliff stepped down from the cockpit, the dock rocking underneath him. He shook my hand firmly.

'Hello, Charles. Hi, Kathy. That's right, ain't it?'

We threw boxes, sacks and cases into the back of the fuselage. Cliff strapped it all down tight under a tarpaulin, and said we should turn around quickly. Kathy and I climbed in. Stella sat alongside Cliff up front. I thought about flying to this wilderness camp, how the planes got smaller with each turn, like Russian dolls. Cliff turned a switch on the complicated dash, and the unsilenced exhausts of the radial engine thumped on the fuselage like a drum. We flew over mossy rocks along the lake shore, so low I imagined I might see a pike in the shallows.

Strangely, the camp was almost empty, but for Cliff and Stella, their son Craig, and a few native Denee, who worked at the camp as guides. All the camp regulars knew that the lake trout were starting to move from their deep, summer lies but hadn't yet reached the rivers. That would make them difficult to find. In a few days the camp would fill again, and rods would fish for lake trout on their spawning run.

We rode out that afternoon with Craig, the place to ourselves. Athabasca seemed vast. I tried to piece together some idea of the landscape we were in, of its scale, of the emptiness – we had flown for thirty minutes from the easternmost point of the lake, yet we remained in the eastern corner. Beyond the islands to the west was an expanse of water with no far shore. You could run an outboard fishing boat for days across Athabasca before reaching the other side.

We came to a reedy bay. Craig killed the engine. The water was dark, but clear. We drifted over deep weed-beds which billowed like underwater clouds in the soft currents. A headland behind sheltered us from the worst of the wind, but small whitecaps came round that tip of rocks and sent rippling waves up into our bay.

Kathy hadn't really fished before, so Craig set up a spinning rod for her. He had a concertina tool-box full of plugs and spoons, rusted hooks, teethmarks across the painted sides of the plugs. He chose a six-inch imitation of a grayling, with a diving vane on the nose. It moved through the water like an injured fish, wobbling and rattling just above the weed. 'Looks perfect,' said Craig, handing her the rod. 'Now just pull back on this bar, throw out the bait, wind the handle. Maybe jerk the rod tip up and down a little to liven it up.'

'As simple as that?'

'Sure. You wait and see.'

Kathy had a take first cast. The fish came and went in one hit, smashing the rod against the gunwales. Kathy looked at the rod like it had bitten her. 'Was that a fish?' Craig nodded. On the feed a pike will hit the lure like a hammer. A hungry pike just explodes with instinct. I think sometimes it's like running your fingers across the bars of a cage, while inside is a beast you just know is going to snap at them, banging the cage with its jaws.

Kathy cast again. I stirred through the box of pike flies I'd tied up for the trip. Piles of marabou feather, tinsel and twinkle yarn, cartoon eyes, fat silver or green bodies. I knew they'd drive these pike crazy. Catching pike with a fly is, as a friend once said, 'the long way round the barn'. You can't crank and lever a fish with a fly rod; a powerful, heavy pike will bend the rod in half. Connecting their primal ferocity to the delicacy of fly-fishing makes the whole thing gothic in a way that is endlessly enjoyable.

It took about three minutes, twenty-six seconds. Bang! Suddenly the rod was alive, the reel grunting like a pig. Line zipped out sixty feet in one surge. The fish was nearly forty yards out from the boat before it slowed. As I tightened the line pressure the pike leapt high out of the water, its whole body charged with electricity. The gills flared. I saw daylight through them. It slammed back through the lake, and leapt again, this time walking on its tail, before falling forwards like a clumsy drunk. I pulled and the fish pulled. I won line, and lost it, until minutes later she lay beside the boat, a huge female longer than my leg, patterned with golden and emerald flanks as though we were looking at the sky through the leaves of a birch tree. Well over twenty pounds. I held her in the water, felt the cold skin and touched the heart of the wilderness.

Kathy had her first a few minutes later. The bay

was full of pike. In the clear water we could see them smash into the lures right up by the boat. The bigger fish were hooked further out. If they followed and saw us they'd turn away. But two or three times as I wrestled smaller pike through the waves I noticed dark shapes moving below them, and once I saw a dark shadow half the length of the boat sliding along the lake bed, latent with menace. I started to wonder how big you'd have to be to feel safe down there.

Later that afternoon in a different bay, I saw a pike's head appear from the shadow below a shelf of rock. It stopped short of the fly, then flared its gills, sucking the fly into its jaws. That fish was huge, really huge, but I stared at it, frozen. By the time I lifted the rod there was too much slack in the line and I missed the strike.

It was quiet that first evening with just us in the dining room. Cliff stood at the bar and offered us beer from the cooler. The bar doubled as a tackle store. Massive lures hung from the walls behind Cliff, alongside a few snapshots of anglers holding up monsters, the same lures dwarfed in their jaws. Further along the wall was a shoal of stuffed fish, not in cases, but hanging in the air – a pair of grayling, three or four walleye, two lake trout. And two pike as big as wardrobes attacking startled shoals of baitfish. A moose looked down with dumb bemusement as though it had charged through the wall from the outside, a collection of baseball caps stapled to the boards round its shoulders.

We ate chilli con carne. The talk limped politely from one topic to the next. The next evening was the same. Cliff cracked the odd dry joke. He was tired but dutiful. Me and Kathy got on fine, but she was shy, and I'm never the catalyst for a party atmosphere. It was fine, but quiet. Then Doddy, Penny and Irene arrived. We had our party. Just then I was starting to itch a little. Under my arms at first, then down by my legs. I took a walk outside because the itching was getting worse. Under the dock light I could see red bumps everywhere. I had no idea what they were. But Doddy knew. 'Hives,' she cooed. 'Just wait there, honey, I'm gonna rub something in to make you better.'

'I think it's just that chilli sauce you splashed on your food at lunch, Charles,' said Cliff from behind the bar as Doddy went off to fetch her bags. 'Pretty damn hot, that chilli sauce.'

'It could be anything. What are you allergic to, hon?' asked Penny, soothingly.

'Us!' said Irene, snorting back a giggle. Penny hooted and pushed Irene on the shoulder.

'Behave, will ya? He's English, for heaven's sake!'

'Jees, look at him. He's scared already.'

Cliff had picked them up from Stony Rapids while we were out fishing. Penny was tall, blonde, with long painted nails. She spoke with an accent that filled her words out, like fluffing a pillow. She told me she lives in a dry county and has to make booze runs across the county line. She has a fridge in the yard, so she doesn't have to go inside to fetch a beer when mowing the lawn.

'She does too,' said Irene. Irene was thin with black hair, and laughed a lot. She looked at me as I ate.

'Isn't that cute? Will you look at that, Penny? He's using the curved side of his fork. You know, darlin' I bet you're glad you had that war with us. We're so crude always using the wrong side of the fork.'

By now Doddy had arrived back with some Benadryl. Doddy was larger, with short brown hair and gentle eyes. She looked at me, and rummaged through her bag. 'Got some relaxant here. Gonna rub it into that neck of yours. You look a little tense.' She kneaded my neck like I was a loaf of bread. After that she pulled out two horse-sized pain relievers, and some gel for patients undergoing radiotherapy.

'Don't worry, darlin, we'll take care of you,' said Irene. 'We'll just come and check on you every two hours.' She winked.

'Reckon you'd be safer if a bear came in to look after you,' observed Cliff.

'Hey, hey, hey!' said Doddy to her two friends. 'Look. I've got gloves! Latex gloves!' They all screamed with laughter. Then Doddy fixed me with her big eyes. 'Oh look at you, I bet you're wondering what you did to end up here with three bad American broads.'

The hives were bad too. I lay awake all night, scratching, and turning on the light every so often to see how much worse it had got. By three in the morning I was covered. It looked horrible. But I wasn't going to go and ask anyone for a second opinion. I just looked at the ceiling and tried not to scratch, and the hours ticked past slowly.

In the morning one of the guides boated Kathy and me over to the clinic at Uranium City, an old mining town on the shore of the lake, about twenty miles away.

It was a long choppy ride, and the cool air took my mind off the itchiness. As we approached the cove at Uranium City we saw young kids messing around by the lake. A few hung lines off the defaced rocks along the shore, and all of them turned to watch this boatful of strangers. The white paint told us to 'Fuck off'. Uranium used to be a bigger place, when the mine was open. Now the population is a tenth of what it once was and most of the buildings are empty. What's left is a dusty foreshore town bleeding depression out of every cracked weatherboard and broken window.

Our guide told us how to find the clinic and stayed behind to guard the boat. He said the kids would be all over it if he turned his back. At the centre of the town we came to a crossroads and stood back while quad bikes raced past, throwing up a cloud of dust, a sharp two-stroke jangle cutting through the silence. On the other side of the crossroads stood the town hall. Notices about drug abuse and depression counselling lined the boarded windows.

The nurse asked me what I might be allergic to.

We went through the food I'd eaten, the places I'd been. I mentioned some conditioner I'd used washing my clothes back in Montana.

'I've seen that stuff drive people crazy,' she said. She gave me more Benadryl, some calamine lotion, and told me to wash my clothes out in fresh water. They were kind; they have problems there bigger than tourists with hives.

One morning we all flew out to the McFarlane River, a place where vast inland sand dunes form the delta of a river system as it flows into the lake. I sat co-pilot with Cliff, and worried about his arteries, trying to work out if I could, at a pinch, fly that thing if I needed to. He turned dials and pumped at handles in no discernible order, and I concluded that if his heart popped we were all pike food.

Cliff dropped us off at the mouth of the river. He had boats moored over on the delta, and we followed the river for two miles upstream until it opened out into a pool, so big that it was effectively a lake. Along one side there were sand dunes towering over the water, a hundred feet high. Along the other bank the river seeped through braided channels. We moored by fallen trees, and started to work the water. Irene was in the other boat with Doddy. Her rod was the first to bend over.

'It's just weed,' she said, heaving backwards. The rod bucked at her. A pike appeared on the surface. 'Oh my God it's a fish! Will you look at that?' Hooting with laughter, she cranked the handle of the reel, hauling the large fish at speed towards her boat. Suddenly the pike leapt into the air and shook its head. I could see the red gills flare, and heard the spoon jangling against its teeth. It was a big fish, landing back with a splash which reached Doddy and Irene.

'Oh my God,' said Irene. 'Did you see that? Are these things dangerous? I didn't like the look of him at all.'

Doddy screamed. 'It's a monster, and it's so pissed.'

The two of them screeched so loud the sound echoed off the dunes. They laughed and waved their arms at the angry fish. Irene had stopped cranking the handle, and the pike was spinning in the surface, soaking the two of them.

'Get it in, will ya Irene, before it causes an accident?'

The pool was full of pike. Kathy and I motored around the disc of water, following the wall of sand, stopping to cast under fallen trees or against islands in the delta where the river ran in. The sun shone hard into this amphitheatre of sand dunes and water. Heat built up in the still air, but still the pike came. I hooked one fish which peeled off fifty yards of line, straight through the weeds, unstoppable. Pike rarely run even in open water, but it felt like I'd hooked a skidoo. The fish ran on until the strain was too great. It smashed the twenty-pound line. I never even saw it.

We took thirty fish between us before stopping for lunch, keeping the last four small ones to eat. Using the rocks at the water's edge as a cutting board, the guides cut the fish up, slicing along the ridge of forked bones to take fillets off the top and bottom. People complain that pike are bony. It wasted some of the meat but it had never occurred to me to dispose of all the forked bones so neatly. We rolled the fillets in egg and flour, and cooked them in hot oil. We ate the fish with chips and ketchup sitting in the reflected warmth of a sixty-foot sand dune. I sat on the edge of the conversation, soaking up the heat like a reptile, thinking about how no chef in the world can improve on the way ordinary food tastes when you're outside in the middle of nowhere. The ladies were on about Diet Coke, and weight loss and what life was all about, especially when it was cut short. I discovered bit by bit that Doddy had come up here with her friends to scatter her husband's ashes on one of the outlying lakes. Why here, I asked? It was his favourite place. He came up every year. The following day Cliff would fly them up to this special lake in the hills, and the three of them would say goodbye.

On the last day a deep mist settled on the lake. The water was flat as a frying pan. We ran across the eastern edge of the lake, the wake of the boat splitting the flat calm. We stopped and the wake settled. We could see for twenty yards in a perfect circle round the boat. Sound was magnified in the still, damp air. Out in the mist, beyond sight we could hear pike feeding, slamming against the surface. Then one struck close to the boat, a boil on the surface the size of a paddling pool. I made a cast close to the spot. The white feathers of the lure flickered through the surface and vanished. The line pulled away sideways, cutting a V across the lake. I let the fish run a few yards, then pulled hard on the line to set the hook. The loops of fly line loose on the deck of the boat snapped up, spinning round the butt of the rod. I released the loop as the rod bucked down, just in time, then the lake erupted. A massive hen pike held vertically over the surface, straining against the leash of line. She'd soaked us through by the time we got her aboard, plunging down four times from the edge of the boat, each time the tail beating at the surface, showering water across us.

Later I sat with Cliff and Kathy in the dining room, looking for a hole in the weather through which Cliff could fly us in his shiny vintage plane. Doddy, Penny and Irene were staying for a few more days and were out fishing, beyond the headland. As I stood on the dock before we took off, I heard a distant scream, hoots of laughter.

Sitting in the terminal hut back at Stony Rapids I thought about Doddy's husband, and what it's like on the edge of civilisation, up against the vast emptiness. I copied down the sign for Scott's General Store – 'Groceries confectionery gas bar fishing hunting camping tanned furs raw fur buyer expediting services northern memorabilia bombardier ski-doo dealer sales and service chain saws' – and climbed aboard a slightly bigger plane.

David Beckham is the Best

AT FIRST THERE IS NO NOISE WHEN I KNOCK ON HER door. Ronnie is waiting in the garden with Birch and Marc. He's telling them, 'You wait, she's great, you wait and see.' They don't really know what to expect. I look up the wooden stairway. I think she must be in because her clogs are at the foot of the stairs. But the door at the top is closed. Round the side three scrawny hens peck at corn and scratch at the soil around the vegetables. I call hello, and the window upstairs is thrown open.

Mrs Slivo leans out, pissed off to be disturbed. She looks down and sees me. 'Charlie!' She sees the others waiting nearby. She disappears. Only a few seconds later she is at the top of the stairs with a bottle and four glasses. 'Charlie! Ronnie!' More words in Croatian that I can't understand. She climbs down quickly, leaning her weight back because the stairs are steep and she is a big, fat woman. She gets me in a bear hug. Then Ronnie. I introduce her to

Birch and Marc. She remembers her bottle. 'Oh shit,' says Ronnie. 'This is where the trouble starts, lads.'

She fills each glass to the brim, hands the first to Marc, and gestures for him to drink it fast. Marc knocks it back in one go. Birch studies Marc's face looking for signs of pain. Marc exhales. 'Feee-uuuck. That is good stuff. That is good stuff.' Birch hits his eagerly. 'Jeepers, Charlie. What is it?'

Ronnie and I are loving this.

'Croatian jet fuel, pal. That's the way to start a week's fishing. Shagged before you've even strung the rod up. Ha ha.'

'We're not going anywhere till the bottle's finished. She won't let us.'

By now Mrs Slivo has filled Marc's glass again, and is rubbing his back while he drinks it. She does the same with all of us. The bottle is now half done. That's another two each. Shit. We will all be bombed.

'Good. Is good yes?'

We're nodding, trying to swallow. I pull out the magazine from behind my back. I wrote a piece on the place the first time I came here with Ronnie. I show her the picture of her with Ronnie's head in an arm-lock, then the picture of her house in the meadow beside the Gacka. She gestures to ask if she can keep it. We stay for another ten minutes, until the bottle is dry, Mrs Slivo rubbing and slapping our backs, nodding and saying 'Is good. Is good.' We say we'll see her later, bring her a big fish. My legs feel soft.

Her house is right at the top end of the river. A

limestone escarpment rises steeply from the valley floor. At the base of it is a pond. Watch it for a while, and the flat water surface starts to shimmer. It's vibrating with the force of the springs which feed it. Within ninety feet of the escarpment the water spills from this pond through a line of four derelict flour mills, cascading over rocks and the beams and boards of broken buildings. Then the currents coalesce and the Gacka begins.

It's a big stream from the start, too deep and fast to wade anywhere, but within only a hundred yards another stream has joined it, and further on another, until within half a mile the Gacka is a broad, powerful press of water, easing across the karstic valley.

Mrs Slivo's house is in the meadow below the mills. We can see trout from her garden. It's this upper meadow, where the Gacka starts, the cold, clear water fanning urgently over bright weed, curving through a field of wild flowers and apple trees, framed on each side by the limestone, where the grey trout shimmy nervously over a calcareous white river bed, that keeps bringing me back. I could fish here for ever.

'Drink,' I said to Ronnie. 'It's good. Drink. It'll dilute the slivo. Shit, my head is spinning. I'm floating on that plum juice, like my feet aren't quite hitting the ground.'

The spring emerged cold and clear from under a pile of stones. The moss on the stones was coated with insects. With care I could cup my hands under the surface and get a mouthful without the flies. The water numbed my hands. Ronnie leant against the roadside barrier above me.

'You didn't even drink half the bottle, Charlie, you big girl. I had most of it.'

'That stuff. It's poison. You could run dragsters on that stuff.' I put my hat into the pool, filled it, and put it back on my head. 'Oh that feels good. That feels so good.'

'Charlie. You're one per cent more water than the rest of us. I can't believe how much water you drink.'

'Jeepers, what was that stuff she gave us? She liked you though, Ronnie. She said you were her teddy bear. Reckon you were lucky to get away.'

Two cows looked at us from the shade of the trees a few feet away. Further along the track a farmer was talking to a group of women. He saw us approach, and skipped away from the group to open the gate into his meadow. The women laughed at his exaggerated gallantry. He was tall, but stooped, probably from so many years hoeing his vegetable beds or scything the hay meadow. He had a mop of white hair. He smiled, and his brown skin creased around his eyes, but otherwise his face was set and stark. It was hard like many other Croatian faces. A stone expression that I assumed must hide things I could hardly imagine.

We spoke about this with the Aussie lady on the train. I remember her full and flush face, and weirdly self-contained laugh, but her expression had changed. She was married to a Croat. She was working in Zagreb, following up a few stories. She told us about a teenage boy who lived in the village her husband came from. The boy's family had no money, so when he went out hunting he had to use his bullets well, and get rabbits to eat. He was good at shooting. He fed his family rabbits.

The Serbs came through this village. Everyone ran to the woods on the hill, but the grandfather refused to go. So the boy stayed with him. They heard the voices of the Serbians as they came up the village street. The kid recognised a few as friends from school. He had a good vantage point, and he shot them all. He told the Aussie lady that he knew he wouldn't miss, and asked her if she could imagine what it was like to kill old friends like this. She couldn't. He told her it wasn't good.

This lower run flowed deep behind the farmer's house and alongside two sheep meadows, one grazed short, the other still long and shot with wild flowers. The river knuckles along the far side, feeling its way under the overhanging branches, until towards the end of the first meadow it sounds away, turns a lazy corner, divides around a stand of trees, and runs into a pool where a strip of green weed wafts over the edge of the deep drop-off. Grey trout hang in the eddying boil off this complicated current. I stopped and watched the fish. Ronnie passed behind me.

'Dream on, pal. You catch one of those and I'll eat my friggin' hat.'

He walked on to the channel below where a few trout rose steadily. I waited, studying the grey shapes as they rode the crests of invisible waves, lifting and sinking to pick off hatching olives. I tried my first fly. One of the shapes tilted up, surfing. I tried again, and the shape turned down off the current and out of sight. I waited again, then tried another fly. A fish jinked to the side, as the first reappeared. The rhythm of the feeding fish fractured for a moment. They moved uneasily, then settled. It was difficult to avoid drag across the breadth of these conflicting currents, and the trout seemed alive to the tiniest hint of it.

After some while I tried a small fly tied with hare's ear fur. A trout lifted quickly. I saw a flash of white and struck. I felt the size of it. This was a big fish. It ran to the far edge of the pool and cleared the water in a violent twist, dropped back in again and ran to the head of the pool, curling its body back as it jumped once more, turning around the apex of the hook. I thought it was gone, but the hook held.

The trout swam quickly over the tail of the pool across a shallow of gravel and weed, through the thin water, pushing a wave down ahead. The wave moved with the current, spreading wider and wider until the ripples became parallel. As the fish dropped into a deep hole, it gyrated on the end of the line, running and tiring in shorter intervals until it gave and I slid it up to the bank.

'You tosser!'

Ronnie was alongside me.

'Ha ha! Eat hot lead, doubter. In fact eat your hat.'

We taped my fish at seventeen inches.

It didn't take us long to ask about the war, though it was small talk at first, with Sanya translating – the weather, the journey, how long it was, how hot it was, questions from us about the mayfly hatch, about trout – but Ronnie and I wanted to understand. The war is inescapable. For an outsider its imprint is everywhere.

'Bloody hell,' said Ronnie on the journey down, nodding to the shell of a farmhouse, 'there was a scrap that went on here. Did you see the bullet holes in that building?'

In Otočac deep pitted scars slashed up the sides of houses, bullet holes stitched across walls. 'Why did they bomb Otočac?' Sanya stirred her coffee. 'Because we were at war.' Damir acted as though he couldn't understand, just stared out the window. Finally he said, 'No, we do not like Serbs.'

The talk dried up. We sat in silence. I asked was it true farmers here used dead mayflies to fertilise their allotments? Damir laughed after Sanya translated. Maybe once, he said. But now the mayfly hatch is not so good. He could have meant this year, or in general. I wasn't sure.

We wanted to get to the river, to see the Gacka

properly. Damir's Yugo thumped over the rutted track, Sanya up front, me and Ronnie in the back, knees pressed against our chests. The sun was glancing orange off the low limestone hill to the west and a few mayflies danced in the headlights. Four men leant on the bridge handrail, looking downstream. A couple of snotty kids ran past us as we climbed out of the car, kicking a ball ahead of them. The other side of the river a flock of sheep grazed the edge, their bells knocking arrhythmically.

Below us a large trout moved a ripple that spread across the flat water to the edge of the stream. Big caddis flies jigged about on the surface, cut across the river, chasing a wake out behind. Hundreds of flies. Damir was next to us now, nodding. I pointed at the river below. 'Big fish.' 'Sure,' said Damir, shrugging as if that was obvious. 'Now catch them!' He laughed and walked back to the car.

The evening caddis hatch does not get easier with time. We fish at Toncin Most, or two bridges upstream where the river runs in a broad canal down to a line of poplars on the far bank. A wooden punt lies half submerged against the reeds on the near bank, hasn't moved in years, and working up from here I cast up under the poplars, looking for rising trout as the sun fades and the land turns black.

A local angler told me that the big fish only come out after dark, trout two and a half feet long, smashing sedges in the pitch black. I haven't caught one yet, but we've seen them. Upriver from this higher bridge, the stream turns and runs through a shallower reach, the river bed rising and falling like furrows of sand on a beach. A telephone line crosses the river and under it we saw a brown trout that big, maybe bigger. Right at the top in the sheep meadow I found a wild rainbow trout tucked against the roots of an alder. It was over ten pounds. 'The biggest friggin' trout I've ever seen,' as Ronnie put it.

On the flatter water by the poplars, as the light fades, the fishing is marginally easier. Trout pick off weak or spent sedges, and if the pattern is right, and I find an angle which cancels the drag, I'll pick up a fish or two. But at the start of the hatch, caddis pour off the riffles above each bridge. Trout go crazy for them, hitting the surface hard all over the place. Watch one piece of water for a few minutes and you'll pick out the best fish, maybe even a big wild brownie. Then cast. Cast again. Again. Again. Why didn't he take that? What was wrong with that? Again. Change angle. He's stopped rising. Move away – he's started again. Move back and now your first cast puts him down. Hell. What is wrong with these fish?

It'll go on like that all evening.

Eventually you'll work out – or if you've come back, you'll *remember* – they only take the dancing sedge, the sedge that's doing an Irish jig across the surface. It's impossible to make an artificial do an Irish jig. You'll only catch them by fluke. Ronnie thought he'd cracked it the first evening. In the last half-hour he got up behind some big fish, and caught two of them. 'You've got to sit on them to get rid of the drag.' He was right, but when it's dark some of the sedges are spent. Try when it's bright and they're dancing. When it's bright and they're dancing you're smoked.

This time Birch calls over the river. 'Hey Charlie, catch a hold of this.' Birch can cast. He throws the line clean over. I pick up the end, wondering what he's planning. 'Lift it high, climb up the bank a bit, back up, back up. There.' He's tied ten feet of nylon hanging off the fly line, a caddis fly on the end. 'Now let's jig the thing up and down. We'll catch one of these fish, Charlie!' But the bailiff shows up, clattering on to the bridge on his smoky moped. He takes a look at us and stops suddenly, the front forks compressing hard as he puts on the brakes. He watches. I pretend to be unhooking Simon's line from the tree. I look at the bailiff. He's watching me carefully. 'Big cast. My friend casts too far. He is very stupid.' I tap my temple . . . toc, toc, toc. The bailiff laughs and turns to chat to some other anglers. He knows what we're doing.

The bridge is busy in the evenings. Everyone milling about, talking, laughing, pointing at the fish, watching each other, waiting till the right spot is free, then hurrying to it before someone else gets there. It gets competitive. A fat German came up to me. Ronnie was in the water casting to a beautiful wild rainbow we'd spotted riding the current off the second bridge pier. The drag was a nightmare, and I was up above trying to direct the casts. I was back from the edge, trying not to scare the fish. But the German walked right up to the edge and looked over, spooking the trout. He hawked up some phlegm and spat it into the stream.

'Ha, a big fish? Maybe thirty-five centimetres. It's a little one, that. You shouldn't bother.'

'It's a good fish, but you scared it.'

'A little fish. Once the fish in here were all big. Now they are all tiny. It is not worth the bother any more.'

The fisherman's arrow of time. Things always get worse. I wanted this guy's arrow to bury itself in his arse. I stared at him. He shrugged and went away.

Stand on the bridge for long and you'll hear 'shit' in four languages, everyone having the same trouble with the dancing sedges.

Milan would collect us in the evenings – we didn't have a car. Milan was eighteen, had a Renault 4 pizza-delivery van, a dent for every delivered pizza, speakers the size of coffins over each rear wheel-arch. The thing shook to some crazy Croatian funk as he red-lined the needle all the way from his dad's bar, seeing us standing there in the half-light at the last minute, slaloming left then right, over pot-holes, over the bridge, to a handbrake turn at the far end.

'Want to see me Mika Hakkinen – world rally champion?'

'We've just seen it, pal.'

'Fishing is boring! Why you do it? All the time you just stand . . . like this!'

Ronnie and me took it in turns to ride in the back, sliding around between the speakers. Milan is the only one at his dad's place who can speak English. With his dad and the waitresses it's sign language, smacks on the back, much slivovitz.

'So Milan, if it isn't fishing, what is it?'

'What?'

'What's better than fishing?'

'Better than . . . ? Everything!' he laughed. 'Everything is better than! Nothing is worse!'

'OK. OK. What do you like?'

'Girls.'

'Sure, girls. Everyone likes girls. What else? Besides girls.'

'Motorbikes. Football.'

'Ducati?'

'Yes, Ducati.'

'I have a Ducati.'

'How can you fish and have a Ducati? It makes no sense.'

Ronnie chipped in. 'Football. OK, Milan. What team? Croatia has a good team.'

'Yes, but Man United are best. David Beckham. He is best player in the world. David Beckham is the best.'

'David Beckham is a poof.'

'What is a poof?'

'You know. A big girl's blouse . . . girlie under-wear . . . knickers.'

'Girls' underwear? Ha ha! You are wrong. Beckham is the best player in the world for sure. He is my hero. How can you say he is girls' underwear?'

'Don't worry, Milan. Ronnie probably supports some unpronounceable parade of jocks. Hibernian Breeches or something. Anyway, football is worse than fishing. Nothing happens in football . . . all crescendo and no climax. Once in a million years someone scores!'

'You see me play in Otočac. I score all the time.'

The heavy lady leant against her fence watching the chickens. She looked up as we came round the barn. She had coconut skin, a black scarf. She smiled and gestured for us to cross her garden to the river. We nodded thank you and stepped around the vegetable beds and through a gap in her fence. The river curved around the house and orchard. A grey fish snaked back and forth across a clear patch in the weeds. A radio was playing somewhere inside the house. We walked down across the meadow until we were below the fish, and sat on the bank to decide how to go at it.

A caddis tumbled off the surface, and the fish cut to the side under it. We tried a caddis. The trout didn't react at all. We tried again with a dry fly and then a small nymph. The farmer, I guess the coconut lady's husband, was cutting hay under the trees. He put down his scythe, and came over to us. He looked at the fly on my line – I'd changed back to a small caddis tied with duck feather – and shook his head. 'This, nein, this, ja.' He pointed into my fly box at a peeping caddis with a split-shot tied to the head. I knotted it on and said thank you. He went back to his scythe. I took the fly off again after he'd gone. Everyone was telling us to fish with these bombs.

I watched the fish. It darted to the side, dropped down the run and began working its way back upstream jinking side to side. Sod it. I tied the split-shot caddis back on, and threw it at the fish. A bastard to cast, it landed like a stone, and dropped through the water. I lifted the rod to throw a mend against the flow, the nymph twitched and my fish was on to it. I heard the farmer shout from behind as the fly rod jumped down into a bend. I turned. He had both arms in the air. The fish lifted from the river bed and accelerated over the weeds, tearing downstream, his tail half out the water beating at it like a propeller.

'Not exactly Halfordian, Charlie. Did you see the splash? Why the hell didn't the trout freak out at the splash?'

'Reckon these fish are four feet down. Water's so clear, you can't tell.'

'That's a big trout, Charlie.' Finally we had him. 'Look at the shape of that. You don't get that shape on celery. That trout is eating like a pig. There must be some food in there.'

Milan arrived to drive us to Plitvice. We drove

over the pass, and bought honey from a farmer who set up stall at the roadside. We saw more burnt-out buildings, perforated with bullet holes.

'These buildings, Milan,' asked Ronnie. 'Some are shot to pieces, some are fine.'

'These are Serbian houses. It is sad. Everyone was friendly, then everyone was killing each other. Anyway they started it, and now they will not be welcome back. Some are trying to come back. They have no money in Serbia. So if they come back out here in the country people will ignore them. If they try to go to Otočac, it would be bad. Maybe some people would kill them.'

It was time to change the subject.

'It's good of you to drive us everywhere, Milan. What can we give you? A fishing rod?'

'Ha ha, please no. Not a fishing rod.'

He thought for a while.

'Yes. One thing. A David Beckham number 7 shirt, with short sleeves.'

I ordered one when we got home. I mentioned it to a friend who knew Beckham's PR agent. He told me he'd get it signed. It took months. We took it back a year later signed 'To Milan, best wishes David Beckham.' Milan didn't take it off for two days. He wore it to bed. He wore it playing for Otočac, and scored two goals.

The last day we drive up to the mills to see Mrs Slivo, to catch trout in her meadow. I stand on the

broken piers of the flour mills and take pictures of
Marc and Birch fishing the pool where the currents
meet and the Gacka begins. Marc runs a nymph
through the pool. I watch him though the viewfinder,
Mrs Slivo's house on the bank behind, the Gacka
curving away through the perspective of the frame
to a vanishing point of bright green and specks of
fiery colours. The sky is pure blue. Marc's rod jumps
alive, the line catches sunlight and a small trout
bursts into the frame, splashing across the pool
towards him.

Our lunch consists of heavy Croatian bread, slices
of salami, bottles of Orangina. We find a spot where
we can eat and watch the river. We've fished everywhere. This is the best place by far. But Birch has
seen a tributary he'd like to try before we go. A
pretty stream that twists tightly through an unkempt
meadow near a place we call 'street bridge'. I know
the Croatians keep most of the side streams as conservation areas but our map is ambiguous. As we
study the map we hear the bailiff's moped farting
down the hill, switching left then right, until he is
at the mills below us wondering where we are. We
wave and call him over, offer some salami, some
bread. He checks our permits – the sixth time this
week – punches a hole in each of them, and we try
to ask about the tributary. He speaks no English,
only a little German. Birch speaks German, but the
conversation gets Babylonian, all nodding and shaking and pointing, until Birch thinks we can fish it, I

think we can't but am happy to try, and the bailiff looks pleased that we understand. We give him the rest of the bread and salami, and take off for the stream, stopping only for a coffee at a roadside café.

It's a beautiful stream, only a few feet wide, but carrying a heavy flow of clear water. At each turn a deep pool or undercut troughs at the edge of weed-beds. Birch fishes below the road while we watch from the bridge. He throws a heavy nymph up over the gravel riffle, trying to drop it into the deeper water under us. We can see a big fish. It's shifting uneasily around the pool, but at the first cast he charges the nymph, turns and hugs the gravel.

'You missed him.'

Birch keeps trying.

We see three big fish in the pool above the road. Ronnie decides to fish for them, and I walk upriver through the meadow, casting into the pools and against undercut banks, standing well back, my line falling across the dry grass. I catch a couple of small brownies, but turn when I hear the bailiff's moped. I can tell right away from his body language I'm in the wrong place, and start winding in just as Marc shouts over, 'Charles, you better get back here.'

I walk back looking as apologetic as I can. The bailiff nods severely, indicating that I am forgiven.

'We're fishing the conservation zone. He's a bit pissed.'

Unfortunately Ronnie has hooked a good trout in the pool above the bridge. The bailiff watches him like a headmaster watching some kid painting on the walls of a new classroom block. But Ronnie can't get the fish in. It's a rainbow and won't tire. Every time he steers it towards the edge it kicks and the reel fizzes out a bit of line, until the noise becomes awful. None of us says a thing.

Finally Ronnie gets the fish in, and Birch jokes that Ronnie is a naughty boy. We laugh and the bailiff's stern face softens just a little. Then Ronnie walks over, and continuing the naughty boy joke, turns and bends over. 'Ha ha. Naughty boy. Smack, smack.' It seems funny until we realise that the bailiff doesn't understand. He looks at Ronnie without a trace of comprehension or amusement, and the moment seems suspended in time. Ronnie stays there, still bent over, slowly realising that his conciliatory joke is going down badly. Before anyone can clarify the gesture with a mock smack, Birch steps forward and grabs Ronnie's haunches, pantomiming heavy pelvic thrusting and roaring with laughter as he does so.

Marc and I walk to the far side of the bridge willing the moment to evaporate. The bailiff looks like he wants to get away. Birch's pelvic motions subside as he at last becomes aware that the bailiff still isn't smiling. He tries to compensate, full of bluff, asking if the bailiff will show us the correct place to fish. He gets the bailiff to pose for a photograph, and then says to him 'You will come with us?' The bailiff nods, but looks nervous. He gets on his moped and rides quickly across the field. We watch him go. He disappears over the hill. We watch the blank horizon for a moment. He isn't coming back.

'Guys,' says Marc. 'I think we're just about ready for another country.'

Acknowledgements

Vicky for everything.

Jonathan Young and all at *The Field* magazine for encouraging me to write, for sending me fishing, and for publishing my articles. Some of the stories in this book began as commissions for *The Field*.

Ronnie Butler, Richard Slocock, Patrick Lloyd, Rod Hughes, Nick Zoll, Simon Cain, Marc Bale, Jim Babb and the freeze-dried crew, Mark Bowler, Jonathan Young, Tony Ling and Tony Hayter for good company and good days spent fishing.

Tristan Jones, Rachel Cugnoni and Beth Coates for believing in this book and helping me to write it.

Jim Babb, Nick Zoll, and Tom McGuane for well-chosen words of encouragement, and direction. Rachel Thorn for her French.

'London Trout' first appeared, in different form, as

'Trout Within the M25' in *City Fishing* (Stackpole Books). 'Ennui' first appeared, in different form, in *Gray's Sporting Journal*.